Questions and Answers

Questions and Answers

A shorter Catholic catechism

Otto Pesch

Franciscan Herald Press · Chicago

Original edition first published in the Federal
Republic of Germany
© Matthias Grünewald-Verlag, Mainz 1974
This edition first published in 1976
by Burns & Oates, 2/10 Jerdan Place,
London SW6 5PT
and
Franciscan Herald Press, 1434 West 51st Street,
Chicago, Illinois 60609
Translated by John Maxwell
© Burns *&* Oates Limited 1976

Nihil obstat F.J. Bartlett, Censor. *Imprimatur*
David Norris U.G. Westminster, 17 March 1976.
The *Nihil obstat* and *Imprimatur* are a
declaration that a book or pamphlet is considered to be free from doctrinal or moral
error. It is not implied that those who have
granted the *Nihil obstat* and *Imprimatur* agree
with the contents, opinions or statements
expressed.

ISBN 0 8199 0620 4 (USA)

Made in the United States of America

Contents

Simple faith–complicated theology

Sermon practice in a seminary. An aspiring young preacher gives a trial sermon. He does his best to include everything he's heard on the subject in his theology courses. Then his lecturer and fellow students pitch in: "Too complicated!" "Right over their heads!" "Just like a lecture, not a sermon!" "What was the point of all that study?" he demands. "To find out how to say it simply!" the lecturer retorts.

That true story is a useful warning. There is no such thing as a "pure and simple" faith quite free of all theology. Faith has to be expressed, and expressed in words. To do that a man has to use certain words as appropriate, and reject others as quite or more or less inappropriate, to what he believes. In the process he thinks about the nature of faith and what he is really saying. Then he is thinking theologically. He is practising theology.

The early Christians spoke of Jesus as the "Son of God". But why didn't they call him the "Friend of God" or the "Messenger of God" or the "Servant of God"? Because Christians had thought about Jesus and had reached the conclusion that "messenger" and "servant" didn't describe precisely the unique relationship of Jesus to God and God to Jesus.

And so from the earliest times Christians have prayed: "I believe in Jesus Christ, the only Son of God". That sounds like a simple, straight-forward statement of faith, without any complicated theology. Yet there's a lot of theology in it. Especially if you know how much the title "Son of God" had come to mean before there was any Church, and how much had to be taken into account when Christians called Jesus and no one else the "Son of God".

There is no such thing as a "plain, unvarnished" faith — except in the sense of unthinking belief. But thinking about faith can, should and has become more drawn out than is necessary for a man who is looking for salvation and life in his beliefs. People who go beyond those basics are called theologians. They practise thinking about faith as a special form of science or scholarship — academic theology. Theology of that kind can be as complex as any science, especially since Christian belief is as old as it is and getting older, and there is always more to know about it and think about in connexion with it.

In practising this science theologians want to serve their faith. Representing, in a sense, all believers, they seize on and delve into detailed problems of a correct understanding of faith — questions which not every individual is equipped to resolve by himself. In a way a theologian is rather like a motor mechanic who concerns himself with the functioning of a motor car on behalf of a mass of people who can't grasp every minute aspect of a vehicle's operation yet drive one. Nowadays even theologians can't master the whole of theology. Instead they have to concentrate on one particular area and work in conjunction with specialists in other sectors.

Sometimes a theologian's work gets on top of him. Increasingly, the care he devotes to it can take him away from the worries, questions and experiences of the very people he is trying to help with his labours. If a child or an ordinary parishioner asks him a plain question he's often unable to answer it despite all his theological subtlety.

But faith isn't a privilege of theology professors. A child can hold the faith just as well as a scholar. If a theologian really is serving the faith, even in his complex deliberations, it will show in his ability to "put it simply". Often, alas, he's no longer able to do that. His inability is forgiven him if his scholarship is exceptionally fine, of course. All the same theologians should occasionally test themselves to see if their thinking and study have equipped them to "put it simply".

This book is a theologian's attempt to do just that. It must be possible to speak quite plainly about faith and in such a way that the latest contributions of theology are part and parcel of what is said. It's worthwhile trying to do that especially today when so many Christians are suspicious and even frightened of modern theology. Many people think that theologians are the gravediggers of Christian belief. A lot of people are certainly confused.

Anyone who thinks that modern theology isn't a misfortune but a good thing and even a blessing for the Church, is duty-bound to try to get rid of the confusion. We have to create an atmosphere in which people breathe more freely than in the past when someone starts talking about belief and using the ideas of modern theologians. Straightforward talk about faith has to make it clearer than ever before that it is an invitation to become a free child of God.

What I want to do here is to speak about faith in plain language, but without reducing it to nothingness. I have to look at questions of faith not as a theologian would put them but as they're asked by Christian men and women, ordinary concerned members of the Church who haven't read more than one or two if any works on theology.

I have written primarily for Catholic Christians. Nowadays the Christian Churches have to consider the faith together; they have to work together and pray together. But as things are at the moment no one can live a Christian life between or above the Churches. Faith is naturally at home only in a specific Church. That will possibly change as the Churches get closer to one another. But that isn't the case yet. Therefore I have written this book with Catholics in mind, as well as those who are interested in the faith and life of the Catholic Church. That doesn't mean that I attack other Churches or return to the old enmity between denominations. All I am trying to do is to serve a living faith in a living community. Without that, dialogue with other Churches is pretty useless.

1

Is there a God?

Is there a God? That is the first and most important question of the Christian faith. Many people nowadays, even Christians, don't merely ask: Is Jesus the Son of God? Did God really intend the Church to be as it is? They ask whether there is a God at all.

Why should we think that he exists? You don't see or hear him or any trace of him. The world goes its own way. Men have to solve their problems on their own and no God jumps in to get them out when they are up against it. Isn't it out-of-date, stupid, to count on God? Surely we have to think about much more important and solid things? Like how to end the obscenity of war all over the world. How to make sure of peace. How to make the world a more human place to live in. How to stop nature being destroyed. How to overcome disease and unhappiness. For many people who don't believe or don't believe any longer, the question isn't whether they ought to bother about such things instead. They already do so.

God's tracks
Even Christians are often bothered by those questions or others very like them. Yet we still believe in God. If people ask us: Is there a God? should we answer straight off: Yes, there is a God! God is there! If we skirt round it a bit with a "Yes, but . . ." the questioner will think Christians don't believe in God any longer either.

All the same, we are right to wonder whether we're putting it properly when we say: There is a God! or God exists! God isn't a thing like America or radio waves or fresh flowers at the florist's. He is the *personal* God; God the person, who is free. He can love and he made us out of love. He talks to men, guides them on their way, and is active in men's lives. He is alive. He is a living God. And he is alive in so mysterious yet perfect a way that we can't grasp it with our limited understanding.

Why do we believe in God? Because we have happened on his tracks in our lives. We don't see God himself. If we did we wouldn't need to believe in him. "Believing" means holding something to be true and real and trusting in it even though you don't see it and can't test it. God is invisible and hidden. So hidden that it's quite understandable when a lot of people say he just isn't there. But you can see his traces. Of course that doesn't happen automatically. If you go into the forest hoping to catch sight of animal tracks, it's no use looking up into the air as you go along. Anyone who wants to see God's tracks has to keep his eyes open and can't live as if everything were self-explanatory. Things have to strike him. He has to notice that our life is full of puzzles which we can only tackle because we believe in a living God.

There are bright puzzles and dark puzzles. Among the bright ones are some which hit us so hard that we can only be astonished at them. Beauties of nature and works of men: mountains and a technically superb railway engine, ears of corn in a field and a painter's masterpiece, the oceans and an electronic computer, a peaceful yet inspiring country scene, a successful suspension bridge. None of these things is self-explanatory or self-contained or sufficiently described by saying it serves some useful purpose. There is something bigger behind them if there are things which move us so and even overpower us, and when men can do great things. For it's obvious that we haven't made everything ourselves, and we didn't give ourselves the power to do great things. Here we are faced with a mystery that's bigger than we are. That mystery is God.

We also discover his traces in the dark puzzles of our lives: in questions to which we can't find any answers in ourselves — or only poor ones. Why am I alive? Should I be pleased that I'm alive? Why is there so much hatred in the world? Surely everything would be all right if men were just and loved one another? What have we got to hope for that we can be absolutely sure of? Is death the end of everything? Here too we sense God, who can and will solve the problems — for who can accept that everything is in fact futile, that hatred and death have the last word, that there is nothing to hope for, and that everything fine and beautiful in this world is deceptive and superficial?

The good news
We are not the first to discover God's tracks. Men have found them in every age. St Paul is expressing a common human experience when he writes: "For since the beginning of the world the invisible attributes of God, for instance, his eternal power and deity, have been plainly discernible through things which he has made and which are commonly seen and known" (Rom. 1. 20).

Of course you can read tracks wrongly. All human experience wouldn't be clear enough for us if there weren't good news of God in the world —

news which makes us certain that we're not interpreting the tracks incorrectly. That news is in the Bible. When we become certain in our family, through parents, teachers, friends, priests and ministers and the Church, that we should believe in God, that is because this belief depends on the message of Scripture. The Old Testament tells us about the God who made the world and put man here as its master; about God who guides the hearts of men and sheds light on their path; but also about God who lets them walk blindly into misfortune and yet is still there with them. Jesus Christ and the New Testament add new colours to the picture: this is the God before whom a man can open his heart and unburden himself of his worries about himself. A God who is life and who has power over all death. A God who has called men to everlasting joy, if they themselves want that. A God who insists that men should be just to one another, ready to live in peace, and love one another — wherever and in whatever form they are asked to do so.

The answer of faith

We have heard this news. It has affected us. We are convinced by it. But it didn't and doesn't "prove" something to us in the same way that scientific evidence stops speculation. The message about God we find in the Bible isn't the answer to a problem in the same way as a number showing up on the panel of a calculator. The news in the Bible is a message of confidence; it enables us to trust in something. It offers an unmistakably clear answer to the mystery of all those signs and traces in our life which point to God. That doesn't mean that the Bible solves the problem in such a way that afterwards there aren't any questions to ask. What it does is to show us a way of living through the dark patches, with the hard puzzles. And it gives us a firm hope that they won't remain mysteries for ever.

If you believe in God then you no longer live in an unending darkness of unanswered questions, not even when you feel — as you often do — that there is no light at the end of the tunnel. Man's life cannot be mere chance. It cannot be meaningless or superfluous. God has willed and wanted every single man and woman on this earth as an individual. Therefore the history of mankind, however gloomy and confused it may be, doesn't necessarily lead into the abyss. It can become a road to salvation, for God is the Lord of history and gives us courage to work for mankind even when it seems quite pointless. For those who believe in God, bright mysteries, puzzles seen in the light, are miracles worked by an unimaginable love which wants no more than man's happiness and man's response to his Creator.

The living God is behind everything. He never takes his hand away from all that he has made. Surely that is the most meaningful answer to the bright and the dark puzzles which we have to face in the world and in human life. And so we answer: Yes, there is a God. We say that because we believe in him, and we believe in him because we have responded to the news about him and tried it and found that it gives us an answer even though our questioning is not at an end. We can trust in the message we have heard. The right answer to the question Is there a God? is: *We believe in the living God.*

And yet there is a point in keeping to the old answer: There is a God. When two people are in love they sometimes say to one another: I'm so glad that you're alive! What they mean is: You have given my life meaning, value and joy. *Now I know why I am alive!* If it's meant like that, then *There is a God!* is very much the right thing to say. And a prayer which sums up all Christian faith when addressed to God is: *How good it is that you exist!*

2

Is Jesus Christ just a man?

If we're Catholics, we often say as we make the sign of the cross, perhaps every day: "In the name of the Father and of the Son and of the Holy Spirit". By "the Son" we mean Jesus Christ. Christian belief says that he is distinct from God the Father, but one with him in divine essence, power and majesty, so we should pray to him as to the Father.

What do we mean by that? Certainly not that God has a son as human beings have sons, or that God so to speak slipped into human form as if into a suit of clothes and in that way raised this human form (Jesus of Nazareth) to divine status, accepting him as his "Son". People tend to suggest that that is what Christians really believe, and quite rightly find the idea ludicrous and no improvement on many tales of the old gods. That is what some people mean when they say: Jesus is *only* a "son of man" — a man just like us!

"Son of man"

But a well-informed Christian will answer: Well of course that is the most important point when I say that I believe in Jesus as the Son of God — for at the same time I say quite decisively: He is the Son of Man. If you want to understand and explain to others what believing in Jesus as the Son of God means, then the most important thing to consider is his earthly life. He lived as a normal man of his time. He was a member of the Israeli nation. His home was in Nazareth. He was a carpenter by trade — not some kind of posh cabinet-maker, but a skilled labouring man. He was a practising member of the Jewish religious community. He didn't retire into the wilderness but lived among his fellow countrymen, relatives and friends. And among them he ate, drank, celebrated feasts and important occasions, laughed and cried. Sometimes he was very angry and then he would be merciful, loving and sympathetic. And he was a man of integrity. He was loyal to himself and his friends; and it was that that eventually caused his death. So he was a man all the way through. And a thoroughly good man. But what more was he?

First he had something incredibly stirring to say — a message of a kind quite unlike anything that even the greatest prophet before him had announced. What he said was this: "The kingdom of God has arrived. You must change your hearts and minds and believe the good news" (Mark 1. 15). That means: God is close to men — *all* men. Everyone has to know and trust that God is a God for mankind. There shouldn't be any doubt any longer about God's attitude to men.

From this news Jesus drew some quite shattering conclusions as far as human life was concerned. People weren't to be afraid any longer — of God or of men. And they weren't to be concerned about their own lives: that is, they weren't to persist in the fear that in the end everything was pointless. As far as God is concerned even guilt and failure can't stand in the way of his love for us. People have to realize that they are intended for complete and inconceivable joy. They should live now in such a way that others are more aware of that too. Because God loves all men just as they are, there are differences but no barriers between them: no barriers of class, or knowledge, or ability, or virtue. People have to accept even the guilty — for no one is without guilt. Justice, forgiveness and love should govern men's life together and make it whole. That is the nature of God's reconciliation with guilty men.

More than all the prophets

Jesus took the message seriously as far as his own behaviour was concerned. He collected disciples and made them his fellow workers in announcing the good news. They were hardly the kind of people that a teacher of the law or religious leader out to make a reputation for himself would have chosen. They were fishermen: simple country people, provincial types — the kind people rather looked down on.

He went in for eating with rejects: with fast women, shady business types (customs men) — and he told others to do the same. He offended against conventional standards when they hit the poor hard: the sick for instance, who had to be looked after on the sabbath as well. He went into the temple and attacked the whole system of Jewish religiousness as contrary to the will of God. He made it clear that you couldn't buy God's good will. Men had to learn to believe that God was close to them without their having to help him along.

That was more than anything the prophets of Israel had said, yet it was in line with all their pronouncements. At first, in fact, a lot of Jesus's contemporaries took him to be a new, pretty powerful kind of prophet. But there was a difference. Jesus claimed to be more than all the prophets and teachers before him. A teacher of the law would say: *Moses* said . . . A prophet would say: Thus saith the *Lord* ... But Jesus, without making any comparison and without any appeal to a higher authority declared: Truly *I* say to you.

And there's more to it. Whether we enter into the rule of God or the "kingdom of God" announced by Jesus depends on what *attitude* we take to *him*. That is particularly clear from the sermon which Jesus gave in his home-town of Nazareth (Luke 4. 14-30). Jesus explains: I am the one in whom the promise made by the prophets has come true. His audience believe not a word of what he says — and in Jesus's eyes it is sheer unbelief that prevents him from working the same miracles in Nazareth that he's managed in other towns. Only someone who follows Jesus, joins up with him, in faith at least, and often directly by sharing his wayfaring life, is going to experience the promised nearness of God.

Finally: when Jesus speaks of God the Father, he never puts his audience and himself into a united "Our Father", but distinguishes between "your" Father and "my" Father. Men are the children of this Father, but he alone is his "Son".

The "Son of God"

Those who first heard Jesus preach soon understood that *either* they accepted that fantastic claim and trusted completely in everything he had to say, *or* that he was a blasphemer and con-man extraordinary. Those who didn't believe in him acted accordingly by arresting him and bringing him before their own court for blasphemy, and before that of the Roman occupation forces for causing unrest, and then had him executed. They seemed to be right. Nothing happened when they mocked him as he hung on the cross: "He saved others, he cannot save himself".

We know what happened afterwards. The despair of the disciples, who had given up all hope (Luke 24. 21), didn't last long. He appeared to them as the living one, the man raised from the dead.

Then they tried to think how best to express what could be thought of Jesus. They called him the "Son of God"; they acknowledged him and prayed to him as the "Son of God". Of course we can say in other ways what they meant by that, but that was the precise term for their open acknowledgment of belief as well as for preaching their faith, as it still is today.

Jesus had already indicated to his audience that that was the right kind of name. There are several points in the gospels where Jesus calls himself "the Son" or where others ask themselves or him whether he is the "Son of God" (e.g., Matthew 16. 16; Mark 14. 16; Luke 1. 32). If he calls God "his own" father so emphatically, how can it be wrong to call him the "Son of God"?

The title meant a lot to the Jews and to the pagans — men living in the world of Greek and Roman culture. Jews thought when they heard this name of the mysterious and wondrous king who the prophets had foretold would rule in the coming age of salvation, when God would banish all that was evil in the country and throughout the world, and make everything whole again.

The Greeks remembered their epics of Gods and heroes which talked of "sons of God" and also of gods who came to earth in human shape. But of course neither the Greek nor the Jewish idea of a "son of God" fitted Jesus.

But one thing was clear to everyone when Jesus was called the "Son of God": Jesus was something quite special. He was more than a man. It was unusual provocation to apply this title to Jesus. For with it Christian belief abolished all the magnificent or elevated ideas which the Jews and Greeks had formed of the "son of God". The "Son of God", said the Christians, is none other than the despised, persecuted and executed Jesus.

It is rather the same when Jesus is called "Lord". The Old Testament in the Greek translation produced before the time of Jesus calls God by the same title. Among the Greeks "Lord" was the title of a divinity. And so the Roman emperor had himself called "Lord": because he claimed divine respect and therefore martyred the Christians when they opposed him by declaring that only Jesus was "Lord".

The mystery of Jesus

"Son of God" is the right term to use nowadays to sum up our faith in Jesus. As far as human comparisons can picture anything, the phrase expresses the fact that Jesus and the Father are of the same essence – the same "being". At the same time it is clear that the Father and Jesus are not simply the same person, as if the *Father* had shared our earthly life in Jesus of Nazareth. The authors of the New Testament are much more emphatic and exact on that point than we tend to think. When they say "God", they always mean the Father. Jesus is the "Son", the "Anointed" (= "Christ"), the "Servant" of God. For Christians he is the "Lord". In spite of his "oneness" with the Father, Jesus is in a sense apart from him, for he prays to him. On one occasion he says something which has always given Christians, who acknowledge him as the only-begotten son of God, some trouble: "The Father is greater than I" (John 14. 28).

In short, the name "Son of God" means: Between Jesus and the Father there is a unique relationship of trust, surrender, and standing up for one another. Therefore Jesus can also act on behalf of the Father. What he says and does, the Father says and does; and whatever the Father intends for mankind, he does through Jesus – just as in ancient times great lords and kings called their representatives their "son" In this sense

12

Jesus wants to take all those who believe in him into his special son-relationship with the Father. What he is *essentially,* in his very essence, as the Son of God, is something that no man can ever attain to. The difference between "my" Father and "your" Father will never be removed. But in his living *relationship* to the Father, men should follow — are to follow — Jesus. Paul says: "For now that you have faith in Christ Jesus you are all sons of God" (Galatians 3. 26). And when Jesus is accused of having blasphemed by making himself a god, he defends himself by reminding people that the psalms have already said of *men*: "I have said ye are gods" (John 10. 34; Psalms 82. 6).

The title "Son of God" therefore expresses most aptly what we say Jesus is. At the same time it shows more clearly than all other names of Jesus that we shall never comprehend the *mystery* of Jesus. For "Son *of God*" is no one other than Jesus, "Son of man", the *crucified* Jesus. You may think that the term "Son of God" could give rise to misunderstandings nowadays. But doesn't that happen whenever we talk about something unique? The best way to cut out misunderstandings is not to discard a name which is meaningful in itself, but to make clear what is meant by it. The best way of excluding misunderstanding is always to remember what incomprehensible things are summed up in the acknowledgment that Jesus of Nazareth, the Son of man, is the only-begotten Son of God. Until now no one has found a better name, one which leads to less misunderstanding and nevertheless includes everything we can possibly say about the mystery of Jesus. Therefore we pray in our creed: "I believe in Jesus Christ, his only Son, our Lord . . . born of the Virgin Mary".

"The Word became flesh"

The New Testament offers some help in this matter. In the introduction to the Gospel of St John, Jesus is called the Word who became flesh (John 1. 14). The same extraordinary contradiction found in the name "Son of God" recurs here: "Son of God" is the crucified Jesus. "Word of God" is the "fleshly" man Jesus of Nazareth subject to the fate of death. What is in question is the same profound mystery: God who is set above the world and mankind yet has them constantly in mind and care, the Lord of his creation and his creatures, has not only made a gesture of ultimate love towards rebellious mankind (something incomprehensible enough in itself), yet remains the God set above the world. "In many and various ways God spoke of old to our fathers by the prophets; but in these last days he has spoken to us by a Son " (Hebrews, 1. 1-2). God has assumed the shape of a servant proper to our existence. He has become a man, obedient unto death, even death on the cross (Philippians 2. 6-8).

3

Did Jesus really rise from the dead?

If we look for the first time at photographs of someone we know well, we often say: That's him (or her) exactly (or words to that effect). If we look a bit closer, we have to admit: No, even the best photo can't show us him as he really is.

It's the same when we look at one of the numberless pictures of Jesus's resurrection produced during all the centuries of Christian art. At first we say: Yes, that's just right. As with the question: Is there a God? — as soon as we're asked this one, we should answer: Yes, he rose from the dead. "The Lord has risen indeed, and has appeared to Simon!" (Luke 24. 34). That is the right response to someone who asks what we believe about Easter. If we add a "Yes, but . . .", we make our belief no clearer and scarcely more attractive.

Jesus is quite different
Should we really think of the resurrection as we see it in paintings? The Easter reports in the New Testament leave no room for doubt that Jesus didn't rise up as people wake up from sleeping and then carry on their life as usual. And it wasn't as we are shown in pictures of the dead being brought to life by Jesus; for the people he raised up died later on. The Bible says of Jesus that "being raised from the dead (he) will never die again; death no longer has dominion over him" (Romans 6. 9). But Jesus's new life goes on under conditions quite different to those existing before-hand. Until then it was possible to approach him and talk to him whenever you wanted — but now he has to "appear" himself and is no longer available as you would wish. Earlier on there was no doubt who was there in front of you — but now you might not recognize him at all, or only after talking to him for some time. And the "apparitions" cease at a specific point, not long after they have begun, when he "ascends into heaven". Now Jesus's body has quite unearthly features: When he "appears"

a closed door is no barrier to him. No one saw how all that began, *how* exactly Jesus rose from the dead, and the Bible doesn't have anything more to say about it.

But how are we to think of his resurrection? All good portrayals of the resurrection paint the resurrected Jesus in an quite unreal light – in a glow, up above the ground, dressed quite differently from those around him – in short, like no one else. That is how it should be. We must always remember that we can have no conception of the resurrected Jesus exactly like our idea of the things around us and which we are used to photographing. Even the terms used in the Bible – "resurrection" and so on – are inade - quate, for they compare the difference between the death and the new life of Jesus to the difference between sleep and waking up again. Therefore the Bible uses different terms for exactly the same thing in other places: for instance when it says: "lifted up from the earth" (e.g. John 12. 32; Acts 2. 33; Philippians 2. 9).

Even if we only sense the new life of Jesus but can't get any real idea of it, we can say quite clearly what his resurrection means for us and our faith. Remember the fifteenth chapter of the first letter to the Corinthians: "For I delivered to you as of first importance," says Paul, "what I also received, that Christ died for our sins in accordance with the Scriptures, that he was buried, that he was raised on the third day in accordance with the scriptures, and that he appeared to Cephas, then to the twelve. Then he appeared to more than five hundred brethen at one time, most of whom are still alive, though some have fallen asleep. Then he appeared to James, then to all the apostles. Last of all, as to one untimely born, he appeared also to me . . ." (1 Corinthians 15. 3-8).

Paul has "received" this text; he cites a "tradition" from the early years of the Church. Although that tradition doesn't hand down many details, it does – in the manner of a confession of faith – says exactly what is at stake. The first point is the clear statement: Jesus died. They buried him. No one can doubt that he died. But God "raised up" this dead and buried Jesus – or at least rescued him from death. That was acknowledged by a limited number of witnesses, for he "appeared" to them, and – obviously just as Jesus wished – they handed that news on, just as Paul is doing now. And so the Church came into being. Everything else that we would like to know and perhaps can know, isn't what is really decisive, essential.

The most mysterious bit of this text is the expression "he appeared". Why doesn't Paul just say: "He came to them again" or "They saw, heard and touched him"? Because the writer wants to stress something very precise: "Appear" is a term which the Bible often uses in connexion with the majesty of God. When we say that the buried Jesus "appeared", we mean: He came, clothed in the majesty of God. That points in the right direction, is saying the sort of thing the gospels indicate: Jesus no longer belongs to our world — not so much because he didn't truly rise from the dead, but because his life is now as inconceivably complete as only the life of God himself can be.

Paul cites the old creed because he hopes to show his audience that they have to correct some false ideas about what happens to the dead. "Now if *Christ* is preached as raised from the dead, how can some of you say that there is no resurrection *of the dead*? But if there is no resurrection of the dead, then Christ has not been raised; if Christ has not been raised, then our preaching is in vain and your faith is in vain" (1 Corinthians 15. 12-14).

That is the core of the matter. Christ's resurrection means hope for our life, subject as it is to death. It even means hope for us when we have to die, just as people had to die before. The two things are so closely connected that Paul can end by saying: If there is no resurrection of the dead, then there is no resurrection of Christ.

That is something incredible that we should allow to pass before our mind's eye only for a second. If that were true, then proclamation and faith would be blackness and nothingness: sheer idiocy.

The last word about God
We have to grasp two things. Without Jesus's resurrection there is no hope for the dead. Any belief that holds out no hope for the dead, or offers no light on the problem of death, is a deception, or virtually so. "If for this life only," adds Paul emphatically, "we have hoped in Christ, we are of all men most to be pitied" (1 Corinthians, 15. 19).

The message of Jesus's resurrection is a virtual touchstone for our whole faith. This is the point where it is decided whether Jesus has brought us more than an improved morality and a few nice or elevated thoughts about God and the world. This is where we decide whether Jesus has something more than all the wise men of mankind up to our own times — all those with good and helpful things to say to us, but who couldn't answer the question of death. Here we decide whether we Christians should really be so despairing, afraid, sad, in fact hopeless, at a funeral, or when thinking of our own death, as those who don't believe in Christ.

Therefore the resurrection of Jesus is the last word about God which Jesus brought into the world. Jesus portrayed God for us as the one who holds the destiny of mankind in his loving hands. How can death tear us away from God? He preached God to us as the "God of the living" (Mark 12. 27). Is death the boundary of his power? He described in lively colours that everlasting joy which awaits us. Is death to have the last word after all? What are we to think of Jesus and his message if he himself was ultimately beaten by death? We might go so far almost as to say: God "had" to raise him up, if God was really behind what Jesus had to say. The resurrection is like the Yes and Amen with which God underwrites the message of Jesus.

The Son of God

Only the Easter news makes it certain that Jesus did not deceive us; that he wasn't a charlatan in his actions and a con-man and blasphemer in his claims. Those accusations brought him to the cross. He took nothing back about his work and remained faithful to the last moment — which isn't after all what charlatans and con-men tend to do. But does that really mean that he was all those extraordinary things he claimed to be? Surely other human heroes have shown a similar integrity, when they were unjustly put to death? Only Easter makes things clear. He who announced the start of the kingdom of God, its rightful messenger, God's representative, who claimed to be the "Son" as no one before had claimed, was not abandoned by God in death, but raised up to fulness of life. The cross is not a disaster, but the place where our redemption is concluded. The whole life, teaching and dying of Jesus are one unique act of God. God himself speaks in every word of Jesus. In every one of Jesus's actions God himself is acting. In Jesus's death, God is one with his Son's suffering and death. Clearly Jesus is not just a prophet but the Son of God.

4

Who is the Holy Spirit?

A few years ago a priest was saying a "votive Mass of the Holy Spirit". Afterwards a woman came up to him and said: "Thank you for saying that Mass. The Holy Spirit is my favourite God!" Is that the right way to put it?

Of course not. We don't believe in "several" Gods, among whom one could be our "special" God. But we do believe in God the Holy Spirit.

The Spirit – person or power?

Of course the Holy Spirit is a person and that person is God like the Father and like Jesus Christ. "The grace of our Lord Jesus Christ and the love of God and the fellowship of the Holy Spirit be with you all" (2 Corinthians 13. 13). "Go therefore and make disciples of all nations, baptizing them in the name of the Father and of the Son and of the Holy Spirit . . . " (Matthew 28. 19). In this and similar texts in the New Testament the Holy Spirit is put in the company of God the Father and Jesus Christ. They are mentioned together. According to John the Evangelist, the Spirit does things which only God himself can do: He is the "Counsellor" and "Helper" of the faithful. He teaches them, guides them into truth, and declares the things that are to come (John 14. 16; 16. 8-9; 13).

But there are a number of places in the Bible where the Holy Spirit is described not as a divine Person but as a divine Power or Force – as the Gift of God to the faithful. He is in Jesus (Luke 4. 16-21).

By his power Jesus drives out devils (Matthew 12. 28). God "gives" him to his faithful (Luke 11.13) He is "poured out" into the hearts of Christians (Romans 5. 5). He comes down to the apostles at Pentecost (Acts 2. 1-4).

But we mustn't set these passages in the Bible that speak of the Holy Spirit as a Person against others that don't. The fact that the Holy Spirit is Gift and Person at one and the same time is as little self-contradictory as the fact that Jesus Christ is at one and the same time wholly man and wholly the Son of God. In both cases we are faced with a great and inconceivable mystery. Once again it is plain that we cannot think of God in too mysterious and inconceivable a way. We might almost say: The less we "solve" it, the more assured we can be that we are dealing with God. And we all know how a person can be a gift for us. We have all experienced saying or at least being in a position to say to someone: "You're a real gift! The fact that you're around gives me strength and courage to go on". If we think of the Holy Spirit in the same way, we are on the right tracks; we are looking in the right direction — even when the mystery isn't solved.

The Spirit in the Church

In general this is rather like the resurrection of Jesus. We can't conceive of it, but we can say what meaning the inconceivable mystery has for us. More important than Who is the Holy Spirit? is What does the Holy Spirit do? The Bible has a lot to say about that.

The Spirit keeps us and the whole Church in the truth. He alone enables us to believe at all. "No one," Paul explains, "speaking by the Spirit of God ever says 'Jesus be cursed!' and no one can say 'Jesus is Lord!' except by the Holy Spirit" (1 Corinthians 12. 3). That means: Whoever has the Spirit cannot be unfaithful, and no one can believe in Jesus unless the Spirit gives him that belief.

The other point is bound up with the foregoing: The Spirit enables us to become children of God. Paul tells us that we have not received a Spirit who makes us slaves once again, who makes us live in fear. Instead we have received the Spirit of sonhood. He enables us to call out: "Abba, Father" (cf. Galatians 4. 6). "Likewise the Spirit helps us in our weakness; for we do not know how to pray as we ought, but the Spirit himself intercedes for us with sighs too deep for words" (Romans 8. 26-27).

The Spirit distributes his diverse gifts in the Church. He gives every individual his special "ability", or "giftedness". No one can have all the gifts and no one should be envious of another's gifts, but everyone with his particular gifts ought to use them to serve his fellow men and fellow Christians. In 1 Corinthians (12) Paul uses the highly effective image of the human body which can only live when it has all its very different parts, *all* of which it needs to function properly; it would be ridiculous to argue, for instance, about which limb is most valuable. Among the gifts of grace of the Spirit is also the gift of fitting someone for the office of leadership in the Church. It would be stupid to say that this gift isn't important. But it would also be foolish to say it is the only important gift in the Church.

The Spirit of conflict

Through his many gifts of grace the Spirit watches over the life of the
Church. One creed calls him the "Lord, the giver of life". The Holy Spirit
keeps us in the truth, but that doesn't mean that he is "conservative". He
doesn't as we are sometime tempted to think leave everything as it was
before. We read in the Acts of the Apostles how the apostles always looked
on their undertakings and starts in the new life as the gift of the Spirit.
And in fact conflicting opinions, arguments and debates about problems
in no way contradict the Holy Spirit. At the meeting of the apostles
usually known as the "council", which discussed the unity or splitting up
of the Church, there was a terrific conflict among the brethren at first. But
in the end they reached a decision. And it was introduced, in spite of the
conflict, with the words: "For it has seemed good to the Holy Spirit and
to us . . ." (Acts 15. 1-29). And Paul, who can write so convincingly about
the Spirit, didn't hesitate to argue with Peter when it was necessary
(Galatians 2. 11-16). We have to remember that nowadays when there is
so much contention in the Church. We shouldn't be afraid of conflict. It
can show that the Holy Spirit is at work. Of course there is such a thing
as an unholy row. But that a particular row is unholy has to be *proved*.
You can't assume because there's a row going on that the Holy Spirit
isn't around.

The Spirit of holiness

It is the work of the Holy Spirit if we become good men; if we make
progress in our moral life; if we drive sin more and more successfully out
of our lives; and if we ourselves become "holy". Paul stresses that when
he's talking about the "fruits of the Spirit". Read the passage (Galatians
5. 22-5), and think what an impressive witness to faith it would be if all
believers opened themselves to the working of the Spirit. It also shows
that in the early Church, in addition to the message of the dead and resurrection of Jesus, the Spirit was the most important news to be announced.
"Any one who does not have the Spirit of Christ does not belong to him"
is another neat way of putting it (Paul again — Romans 8. 9).

Who is the Holy Spirit? If we look at the things he does we shall have
more to say about him. Through the Spirit there comes to be and remains
among us, in the world and in our lives exactly what Jesus Christ brought
into the world. That fits what (according to John) Jesus says about the
Spirit. He so to speak "represents" Christ, or "takes his place" in the
world. We might even say: The Father is God "*before* and *over* us"; Jesus
Christ, the Son of God become man, is "God with us"; and the Holy Spirit
is "God *in* us". Here we enter into another great mystery, one we must
consider in its own right.

5

Is God three in one?

If we look at the sun for a long time we are dazzled. But if we turn our back to it, not only can we bear its light but its brilliance and colour become apparent. It's the same when we consider the question posed here, even though the statement "God is three in one" is an unmistakable part of our faith.

Counting and not counting
At first it doesn't seem very difficult. We believe in God the almighty Father who made all things. Jesus Christ, who told us about God and by his death and resurrection opened up access to God, and brought God close to us, is the Son of God, and of the same nature as the Father. The Holy Spirit is the gift of the Father and the Son to mankind, but he is not a thing; he is a Person, of divine nature just like the Father and Jesus Christ. And yet there is only one God. Jesus referred to this specifically (Mark 12. 29). Paul put it more emphatically (Galatians 3. 20; 1 Corinthians 8. 4-6; Romans 11. 33-6). Other gods are "vain things" (Acts 14. 15; Romans 1. 23. 25; Galatians 4. 8; cf. 1 Timothy 6. 16; James 2. 9). Somehow being-one and being-three must go together in God. Surely the right way of putting it is to say (as we do) that we believe in a three-in-one or triune God?

But then it's rather like the sun. If we look at it too long we go blind. Then we no longer see anything where we thought we would. If we count things in life, they're usually separate: three books, for instance, or three trees or three people. They can be exactly the same kind, but they aren't "one" as God is *one* God. When we start to count God, then we end up on a path where eventually we no longer see one God but start imagining three gods, however hard we try not to.

Some old pictures show the Holy Trinity as three male figures sitting round a table chatting. That's taking it too far. We can't complain about

portraits of Jesus or the Holy Spirit as a dove – the Bible does that too.
But it is usually held to be wrong to portray the Father in human form –
the Father who, the Bible says, "dwells in unapproachable light" (1 Timothy
6. 16). It is quite permissible for modern artists to picture the Father sym-
bolically, for instance by an eye or rays of light.

But perhaps we should stop "counting God" altogether. Then God is
still one, unapproachable, unrepresentable, Jesus Christ remains a mere man,
and the Holy Spirit is a symbolic name for an influence from God, which
isn't however the same thing as God himself. But faith can't accept that.
Obviously we have to count even though we shouldn't. It seems more mixed
up than when we started. Even those nice similes they trotted out in old-
fashioned religion lessons don't help, for instance the picture of the three
candles burning with one flame.

Understanding that we don't understand
What are we to do? First of all we have to understand that we can't understand. Whenever we hear God spoken of as "three in one", we have to
realize that this phrase doesn't enable us to understand something as other
terms do. It is an *abbreviation* which we use to express our knowledge that
we are faced here with an incomprehensible mystery. God is much more
mysterious and inconceivable (un-understandable, even "un-picturable")
than the Old Testament realizes. We learn that from what the New Testament has to say about Jesus and about Jesus and the Spirit.

We must follow the Bible in its treatment of this mystery. We have to
speak of the Father, the Son and the Spirit as "equal in rank" (see Matthew
28. 19; 2 Corinthians 13. 13). We have to *pray* to the Father, to the Son,
and to the Holy Spirit. We do that with every sign of the cross, with every
"Glory be to the Father". Even the creed is constructed in that way. We
acknowledge the equal rank of the divine Persons in confessing our belief
in "God, the Father almighty . . . and in Jesus Christ, his only Son . . . and
in the Holy Spirit".

Understanding more about God and the world
We have to turn our back on the sun and look at all the things that the sun
illumines. All we have to do is to name these three names and to think
what the Bible thinks. Then we shall understand more clearly something
about God and the world. First of all God is not "lonely", shut up in or
sufficient in himself. Of course such an idea must have passed through our
minds – the idea of a God eternally happy in himself, who needs nothing
outside himself. But that is not the God of Christian belief. If it is true
that the Son and Spirit of God are as the Father, then the Father clearly
"needs" the son and the Spirit, in order to be the one God. In God there
is opposition, mutual exchange, community. Surely that helps us to

understand why God did not make man for himself alone, but in community? That helps us to see how only a man who lives in community is the full and true "image of God".

If God is Father, Son and Spirit, then we understand how God can be open "outwards". Because he is "conversation", "discourse" in himself, it is natural for him to bring a creation into being and to include in it an understanding, responsive being.

What is more God does not lose himself when he becomes man in his Son, and when his Spirit fulfils the world. He does not lose himself when he takes this being-like-man as far as death itself.

Finally, we understand that God is love itself. He is only God in that he is joined with the Son in the Holy Spirit, who is love in person. He turns towards men in love, because before that he lived a life in himself that was nothing other than love.

Therefore man is the image of God because he loves. The creation story in the Old Testament shows man as the image of God by enjoying power (Genesis 1. 27-8). Greek philosophers at the time of Jesus saw man's likeness of man to God in human reason, in man's capacity for knowing and understanding. The New Testament sees man's likeness to God in love: "And walk in love, as Christ loved us and gave himself up for us, a fragrant offering and sacrifice to God" (Ephesians 5. 1-2).

Of course none of that would be untrue or any the less true if we knew nothing about the three-in-one mystery of God. But since we know that God is Father, Son and Spirit, we can understand better than before what God intended for the world and mankind, and what he has done with the world and mankind — right up to the death of his Son on the cross.

Our whole belief in God, at once our creator and redeemer, is summed up in what Paul wishes his readers at the end of the second letter to the Corinthians: "The grace of our Lord Jesus Christ and the love of God and the fellowship of the Holy Spirit be with you all" (2 Corinthians 13. 13).

6

Can we believe the Bible?

I have already said quite a lot about the Bible. As far as our faith is concerned, it is "Holy Scripture". Why? Because in it we hear and trace the *word of God* in a binding and reliable way.

The word of God
We know that from our religion lessons at school. But what does it mean —
the "Word of God" in "Holy Scripture"? Our whole faith rests on the
fact that God told the world — his creation — what he intended for it. He
didn't of course do that in the way in which someone shouts down to someone below through a loudspeaker, from heaven to earth. Instead he created
human destiny so that men could sense more and more about him and his
intentions for the world. That is especially true of the history of a specific
people — Israel. It was there that belief in God, which is also our belief,
began. The events in the history of this people: how the notion was first
realized in the families of Abraham, Isaac and Jacob (we call them the
"Patriarchs"); how it grew into a people, was freed from Egypt, founded
a nation in present-day Palestine, that for a short time was a major power
and then again went into decline; how great new powers — Assyria and
Babylon — conquered and made it captive; how it finally returned to its
homeland, without significance as a people and state, but tested and confirmed in faith in God as no other nation roundabout. Israel recognized
God at work in these events and learned to believe in him.

The Old Testament
They related these events from generation to generation, and sang songs
about them. They said prayers of thanks for them, and celebrated feasts
in memory of them, and set up a legal code and a political order that fitted
them. It was some long time before they thought of writing them down —
oral tradition was enough. But finally gifted men wrote it all down.

That was all the more necessary since the bigger the nation got, the more scattered was its life. Things could get distorted in oral retelling. So a set of books came into being which hand down to us the deeds of God in the history of the people: prayers, songs, celebrations, laws and precepts, and much else. And men who felt impelled to call on the people's concience in the name of God (we call them "prophets", which means something like "God's spokesmen") often wrote down their speeches, or others did so, so that their threats wouldn't be forgotten.

All these writings were put into a collection which we call the "Old Testament". In the earliest times they had learned to believe in God from events themselves, from the stories of the old men, from everyday life and the feats of the people. But now they learned it from books.

Everyone who reads them or hears them read and doesn't close his eyes, ears and heart to that reading, can hear them say: I too am invited to believe in this God. What if we follow that invitation? Then the books take on an entirely new appearance. Their existence no longer seems accidental. God himself, in whom they ask me to believe, has seen that they exist for that purpose. In other words: In these books written by men God himself speaks to me and says to me: Believe in me! Trust in me! Just as I was close to my people, so I am close to you. Because the books of the Bible lead to faith in this way, they are the "Holy Scriptures". Because God speaks to us in them, we hear the "word of God" in them.

The New Testament

All that was known at the time of Jesus. He himself lays claim to the backing of "Scripture", "the law and the prophets" (cf. Matthew 22. 40), for it contains the word and will of God. But then he, his life, death and resurrection, his word and his actions, underwent a course similar to that of the events in the Old Testament and the words of Moses and the prophets.

At first people handed down what they knew of him orally. His words were handed on in divine service, in the preaching of faith. Only later did they write down at first a few and then more and more of his sayings, explain his person, and what it meant for believers. Finally, in the hands of gifted writers and theologians, history, word and interpretation were combined in general accounts of Jesus. We call these "gospels" after the first sentence of the earliest of them (Mark 1. 1). "Epistles" or letters were added to the collection by various apostles, missionaries and parish leaders — above all Paul.

In this way a new collection of books came into existence — the New Testament. Just as the people of Israel learned belief in the close presence of God in the history of the people from the books of the Old Testament, so Christians learn from the New Testament their belief in God's ultimate and irrevocable nearness to all men in his Son, the crucified and resurrected Jesus.

The New Testament is Scripture too. In it we hear the word of God as much as in the Old Testament. That doesn't mean that the effectiveness of the Old Testament is cancelled in any way. It is the same God in whose activity in the people of Israel and in whose appearance in Jesus we believe. Both Testaments together, the one as the book of promise, the other as the book of fulfilment, form one Holy Scripture — the basic course, so to speak, of faith and the Church.

The question Should we believe the Bible? is answered. For it answers itself. We believe because the Bible invites us to do so. Without the Bible we wouldn't be Christians at all, because we wouldn't believe without it. It is something like the situation in which we ask about someone we like very much: Should I like this man? If we like him, then we like him, and don't ask again whether we should do so. That's how it is with faith and the Bible. Its word invites us to believe. If we believe in God then we believe. The Bible has so convinced us that we no longer ask whether we "should" do so.

The Bible as a human book

Perhaps one of those last ideas seems a rather lazy way out. That we owe our faith directly or indirectly to the Bible because God's word meets us in it is clear. But that isn't what's at stake in the question Should we believe in the Bible? Instead we want to know whether everything happened just as we read it in the Bible. Above all the extraordinary stories of God's miraculous interventions in the course of events.

We hear sometimes about biblical criticism, and "biblical science", and "exegesis", which compare the reports in the Bible with the knowledge we receive from other sources about the time and environment of the Bible. The conclusion would seem to be: It can't have been like that. History has been mixed up with legend, and a religious interpretation has coloured a straightforward record of facts. Then yet other people come along and try to prove that "the Bible is right after all". We breathe a sigh of relief on hearing that perhaps, and yet we are rather unsettled by all the to-ing and fro-ing of opinions, and worry whether in the end what is most essential in the Bible, all that faith depends on — God, Jesus, and our salvation — isn't affected by the uncertainty.

We have to get something very important fixed in our minds: The Bible contains the word of God, but it is *hidden in the word of man*. The more we take the Bible quite seriously as *a human book*, the better. But that means: Its authors were children of their times. That is shown in the language they wrote, which was spoken around them — Hebrew or Greek. They wrote their books as books were written then. Because at that time people liked well-told stories better than they do nowadays, the biblical authors put stories in their books, or even thought of some themselves, in order to show the more effectively what they wanted to say to their readers.

And of course they wrote their books in order to win people to faith in God, whose actions they reported. Is it any wonder then that faithful interpretation and reportage grew together? Nor is it astonishing that in their books they are all concerned with what people otherwise, quite apart from their faith, thought about the nature of the universe, the end of the world, and so on. They didn't write a modern school text, with as clear sequence or "objective" account using the resources of history and other sciences; and they didn't write a sort of police court record, quite simply because they didn't have any idea what that was. And if someone had objected that they were taken in by legends, they wouldn't have understood that as an objection.

Therefore we can't get the word of God in any other way than in this quite human word of the Bible, which springs from its own time and place. If the Bible were something else, if for example it were written as we wanted it, then faith would never have come to us, and we wouldn't have the Bible at all.

If the biblical authors, so to speak by special enlightenment from the Holy Spirit, had written books in a twentieth-century style, no one at that time would have understood them. No one would have been affected by them. Then no one would have been interested in them, taken them up, written them down, translated them into other languages and spread them about. If that had been the case, we nowadays would know nothing of the Bible.

Therefore there is a very good reason for God's word being put in human words. We should be thankful that it is, and not complain if we who are born later and in another place not only have to translate the Bible, but explain it, and interpret it, in order to understand it properly.

Biblical science

The important thing, which is that we are invited to believe in God, is clear to anyone who reads the Bible with an open heart. But sometimes interpreting details can be hard work. And so biblical science or "exegesis" has come into being as an attempt to work the hard bits out. Naturally different opinions come into play in the process. But that is no reason to be frightened or suspicious of exegesis, as if it could disturb our simple faith. We should of course take into account a couple of simple rules when we hear the latest ideas and assertions of the biblical experts and find them upsetting. We should ask these questions:

1. Is the new idea really a contribution to discussion, or only a question,

or does it pretend to be the whole truth? If the last is true, then be careful. Many theories which claim to be the whole truth are long outmoded. It is incredible that anyone could come along with *one* means of answering all the puzzles in the Bible.

2. If this or that theory does happen to be true, is it still possible to pray to God, to Jesus? If the answer is No, then it turns our belief in God into a product of human wisdom, and Jesus Christ into a teacher of human ideas and a mere good example for our own lives. However valuable all that may be, it doesn't accord with faith. That sort of God and that sort of Jesus just aren't in the Bible.

3. Does the new theory acknowledge the full seriousness of the incarnation — the becoming man — of God in Jesus? Does it leave both aspects — the humanity and the Godhead of Jesus — equally untouched, as I described them in chapter 2? If the answer is No, if one or the other of them is played down, then there's something wrong with the theory, however illuminating it may seem at first.

The books of the Bible

If we know to know more, then we have to go into detail. It is important not to judge in advance. Anyone who has any idea of the hard work of exegesis will avoid any kind of snap judgment. And anyway nowadays there are a lot of very good books on the Bible, which we can read and understand even if we're not bible experts. In these books — and in any really good modern edition of the Bible, we can find out all the essentials regarding the origins of the individual books.

Another word of advice. The books of the Bible didn't come into being in the order in which we have them in any ordinary edition today. They were arranged or collected according to content and meaning. The Old Testament begins with a series of books which treat of the history of the people of Israel. Then come the psalms, more or less the "prayerbook" of Israel, and the "books of wisdom" — so called becuase they teach about God, the world and men. At the end come the books of the prophets. In the New Testament we find first of all the gospels — if we changed Mark and Matthew round, then they would be in something the right right chronological order, for Mark is the oldest of the four gospels. Together with the Acts of the Apostles they correspond to the historical books of the Old Testament. Then comes a series of letters from early Christian apostles and missionaries, headed by Paul himself. Here too not the chronological order but the content and meaning of the books decide the arrangement and the length to some extent. The Revelation or Apocalypse of John is the closing book, the only book which corresponds to the prophetic books of the Old Testament.

The oldest fragments of the New Testament are the two letters of Paul to the Thessalonians — they date from the year 52. But we have to remember that the letters of Paul (and later the gospels too) refer back to traditions, songs, hymns, sayings, creeds, stories and so on, which had been formulated like that in part in the first years after the death of Jesus, and then didn't change any more. The work of the bible scientists helps us to tell how the early Christians — when there was still no "New Testament" — understood and formulated their faith.

Is the Bible so distant from us?

Perhaps some readers will think I want to make excuses for the Bible — because it is so difficult to understand and interpret. That's not the case. I only want to help you to read it properly and not to be surprised that it is a two thousand and more years old book that can't be written as we might wish it nowadays.

In general you don't have to be a bible scholar in order to find out that the Bible is a very interesting book indeed. In one little book called "How to read the Bible" the author asks: "Did you know that the Bible has been translated into more than 1400 languages and that the number of its readers above all in Asia, Eastern Europe and Latin America is increasing? That the Bible took 1200 years to develop and contains songs, letters, similes, folk tales, military reports, speeches, scandal stories, genealogies, love poems, liturgies and even short stories which are the nearest thing to detective novels? That the authors of the Bible represented a range of wholly different ways of looking at the world? That the establishment of the sabbath was one of the first great social achievements of world history, and that the problem of land speculation was already raised in the Bible? That hope in a new society doesn't come from Marxism but from the Bible' That the biblical message first made possible the modern achieving society, but also attacks enslavement by the rat-race principle? That reading the Bible is not so difficult as many think, if you start off the right way?"

Here is a good tip: If you're a parent read the books your children have in the religious education class. In the last few years some good new books have come out. In all the recent ones you should be able to get some neat statement of what the latest biblical research offers.

7

Can Christians make the world a better place?

It's fashionable to ask what Christian belief has contributed to human progress. And in what respects faith has made the world a better place. The questions aren't genuine, of course, for usually the questioner presupposes the answers: Nothing and none.

Faith and progress

It would be tedious to list all the reasons here. We can ask whether the world is better than in Jesus's time. At times, of course, the Church and its spiritual leaders have tried to put every conceivable obstacle in the path of progress, particularly in the sciences, in the belief that those sciences were looking impiously into the mysteries of God and challenging his dominion over nature.

But the sciences and technology won the victory — to some extent against the Church and Christian belief. We realize now that we could hardly survive without science and technology. Nowadays, in fact, Christians try to show that Christian belief far from standing in the way of scientific progress encourages it. But there is a residual inferiority — a feeling that the world has made progress despite faith and is still doing so. The unexpected problems of human social life, produced by the sciences and technology, the new danger that the world could be destroyed by science and technology, now seem to justify Christian mistrust. But the question is still there: Can a Christian make the world a better place? Doesn't everything go along as it's going to, despite him?

Here we should recall two sayings of Jesus: "And while he was at Bethany in the house of Simon the leper, as he sat at table, a woman came with an alabaster flask of ointment of nard, very costly, and she broke the flask and poured it over his head. But there were some who said to themselves indignantly, 'Why was this ointment thus wasted? For this ointment might have been sold for more than three hundred denarii, and given to the poor.' And they reproached her. But Jesus said, 'Let her alone; why do you trouble her? She has done a beautiful thing to me. For you always have the poor with you, and whenever you will, you can do good to them; but your will not always have me.'" (Mark 14. 3-7). Contrary to the disciples who wanted to advocate social justice, Jesus explained: complete social justice, a time when there will be *no* poor people, will never exist in this world. What he says here corresponds to what he says in other places in more general terms: We are not promised a "faultless world".

The commandment of love

But the same Jesus who warned people of illusions, placed the lives of those who believe in him under the dual commandment of the love of God and the love of one's neighbour (Mark 12. 29-31). Jesus says that no other commandment is greater than these two. That is so obvious that we really need no commandment in that respect. If a man really understands in faith that God has come close to him and loves him, then he will answer him in love and thankfulness — otherwise he hasn't really understood it. And if a man loves God in faith, then he will extend this love that he has received to his fellow men — otherwise he doesn't really love God.

You can't love egotistically, for that would mean that it was enough merely to have *received* the love of God.

Jesus himself explained the double commandment of love with the drastic parable of the unmerciful servant who is forgiven an enormous debt yet has his colleague put in prison for the sake of a few pounds. (Matthew 18. 23-5). Anyone who reads the parable carefully will notice that Jesus doesn't refer to any commandment which says that we should forgive our fellow men their debts. All he relies on is the simple fact that a man was himself forgiven a debt, and received forgiving love. That is enough for anyone who car understand to understand.

By "love" the language of the Bible means not just that reality which is known to us all and yet is so mysterious, by which two people feel drawn to one another, accept one another completely and thereby become quite new people. Though of course the Bible recognises that phenomenon. There are love poems in the Bible (for instance the Song of Solomon in the Old Testament). But the Bible acknowledges yet another love, or rather, it knows that people can accept one another in love, and make one another new men, even when they are not at all drawn to one another. Just as God himself has accepted man and made him new. Seen in this way, love simply means being just to everyone, helping others when others need our help, fighting against injustice to others, and above all defending those who cannot defend themselves, not bearing a grudge for injustice suffered, making and keeping peace, even when one is hardly in a position conducive to feelings of friendship; in short, being good even in a world which is often *not* good. Paul puts it like this: "Bear one another's burdens, and so fulfil the law of Christ" (Galatians, 6. 2).

Redeemed world

Just imagine a world in which all men believed in God and his love, answered him with their love and extended the love of God to their fellow men, while behaving justly to everyone and preserving peace. Could anyone then maintain that Christians couldn't make the world a better place? On the contrary. The world would look much better. It would be wholesome and redeemed.

It is precisely that kind of world that God has promised for us on the day of fulfilment, when he will bring into being a "new heaven and a new earth" (Revelation 21. 1).

Of course love and justice are not everything that goes to make up the "new heaven and the new earth". There is the question whether death will also be overcome; whether only those who are living then will be the lucky ones who are to experience the entire salvation of God, or whether all those who lived and died beforehand are called to that bliss as well. This question shows that it is not a human affair, but God's concern alone, to bring about the redemption of the world.

But it is certain that *without* love and peace among men there cannot be a redeemed world. That is so clear that in fact it is possible to think: Surely man's share in the realization of God's salvation is that he, driven on by faith, should spread justice and peace all over the globe? Surely he must do that in order to lay the basis for God's completion of the day of fulfilment.

It is easy to understand why Christians who are quite serious in their faith feel in view of so much injustice, force and unrest, that their most important task is to fight for peace and justice. It's easy to comprehend their suffering and even impatience, and occasionally the impression that they believe they could bring the "kingdom of God" through their own efforts.

But the world of the Lord breaks through that kind of confidence: "The poor you always have with you". He warns us against illusions and deceptions. On the other hand, all that burning desire for peace and justice, despite all illusions, is much more Christian than the superficial and fake piety of putting one's hands in one's pockets and leaving the world's fate to God. Even when he believes, man isn't so good that God hasn't much to do through him before his egotism is quite extinguished and he is wholly ready for love and peace. But nothing will happen unless the believer makes an effort. A Christian cannot lead a completely redeemed and perfect mankind into a wholesome world, but he can make the world a better place to live in. Wherever a man is really a Christian and lives as a

Christian, a bit of God's redemption is already apparent, and men so to speak receive a prospectus of what God has planned for all men and the whole world. And this particular prospectus is not, like some advertisements, better than the reality to come, but a long way behind it.

A beginning to redemption
We shouldn't feel cramped by questions such as: What has belief contributed to human progress? We should simply live what we believe. That goes for our attitude to our own life. It goes for our attitude to people round about us: our family, relatives, colleagues, and neighbours. It goes for our relationship with people a long way off, who can only survive by our help. It is one of the most outstanding achievements of our time that help can immediately be given even a long way off, when people are in need almost anywhere in the world.

For Christians sharing in that kind of aid is an obvious duty, irrespective of who organizes it, so long as it is well organized and the money doesn't go into the wrong pockets. Finally: Love, peace and justice refer not only to men but to "institutions" — the organized means by which human beings live together. Institutions too can be unloving, unjust, repressive or offer room for love, act justly and with a liberating effect. Christians are not to think that they've done enough when they are good to their fellow men, but take no part in politics, economics and social life, which can produce continually new injustice and repression.

A Christian should lead the world and his fellow men to Christ — "christianize" them, as they used to say. But that doesn't mean that he has to take care that the office holders of the Church, the bishops and priests, should have as much influence as possible, wherever possible. We know nowadays that that awakens suspicion and doesn't contribute to the popularity of faith and Church. Christianizing the world merely means making it better. It means bringing love, justice and peace wherever we can in our private and public life.

Has so little happened?
When looking at the past we shouldn't seal our lips. Of course we should search our consciences about the opportunities for making the world better, the Church and Christians have passed up, and the opportunities they have taken to make it worse. But who in the West impressed it on men that they should care for the poor, that all men are equal before God, that peace and reconciliation are better than war and vengeance, that everyone has a right to a just wage? Who founded the first hospitals, established schools and universities, brought about free marriage and cared in politically distressed times for order and security? It is good that nowadays all this is

no longer, or no longer the sole, concern of the Church but of the State and its citizens. Yet in so many "secular", worldly things, such as the "human rights" proclaimed by the United Nations, the "Red Cross", the convention on the treatment of prisoners of war and much else, we recognize the influence of Christian belief. It is shown in the simple fact that all that is far from self-obvious in countries without a Christian tradition.

Do non-Christians do more effectively than Christians what Christian faith demands? Sometimes that is the case, to the shame of Christians.

8

Does morality change?

We constantly read in newspapers and magazines that if we want to tackle some problem effectively we shouldn't trust in an out-of-date morality. The criticism is usually directed against Christians who stand in the way of progress. But are we enemies of progress, merely because we think that moral values and demands shouldn't change arbitrarily?

Something has changed
Sometimes old people, with the bitterness or humour of the wise, remark how the Church, priests and religion teachers repressed them when they were young and put the fear of God into them, whereas modern priests and teachers seem to spend their time knocking the Church for being out-of-date.

Older people often cite the sixth commandment in this connexion: chastity and modesty. An incredible number of things which in the past were thought of as sinful and even as grave sins are now — even at the higher levels of the Church — considered natural, healthy pursuits in fulfilment of the creative will of God.

If today a slave or serf — if there are any still — ran away from his master, everyone would say: Quite right! No one should enslave another man. But the apostle Paul sent a runaway slave back to his master and wrote the master a letter — the letter to Philemon — to say he should prefer mercy to justice. Paul thinks that slavery is permissible, yet that the master shouldn't forget that his slaves are also his brothers in Christ.

Because there is an injunction against it in Scripture (Exodus 22. 24; Psalms 15. 5; Ezra 18. 8), until the eighteenth century it was considered to be against the law of God to demand interest. Only in 1745 did an encyclical of Pope Benedict XIV's explain that not all interest was exploitation of one's neighbour's need — the ground for forbidding it in the Old Testament. Not until the twentieth century did the Church give up its opposition entirely — the end of a resistance once supported with dire ecclesiastical penalties — even though in the meantime interest had become a normal feature of economic life.

Halfway through the last century, Pope Gregory XVI condemned vaccination as an expression of doubt in divine providence, Right into the present century anyone who worked for social advancement ran the risk of being a rebel against the will of God. What else could it express than dissatisfaction with the status accorded one by God's wise ordinance? And do young adults nowadays ever have a bad conscience because they quite rightly want to lead their own lives, yet remember that they are bound to obey their parents as long as they stay in the parental home? The older generation thought unconditional obedience to one's parents was a divine commandment.

It isn't so long since older married couples thought they were sinning when they made love, for they had been taught that *any* sex in marriage had to be backed up by an intention to have a child, and only accidentally could there be none. If it was absolutely certain that no child would result — as with older people — then they ought not to make love at all. It wasn't until 1931, when Pope Pius XI issued his encyclical *Casti Connubii,* that this fear of many older Catholic married couples was removed. He pointed out that marital union not only served the generation of a child but was also meaningful as an expression of love.

Loving God and one's neighbour

1. Moral views — more exactly views regarding what is morally requisite or not allowed, have changed in the course of time and are still changing today.

2. On grounds of faith we already accept many such changes. At most we complain that people didn't reach a better insight into things at an earlier stage.

When there is argument about what is requisite and what is forbidden, and whether an earlier, contested moral demand is still valid, go carefully at first. What now seems self-obvious was contested in the past. Surely what is contested today could be generally accepted tomorrow. The most important thing is to decide what has to remain whatever happens, and what standard enables us to distinguish between a right and necessary, and a false and arbitrary change?

Remember the double commandment of love of God and of our neighbour which Jesus, referring to the Old Testament, said was the greatest of all commandments. "On these two commandments depend all the law and the prophets", he insisted (Matthew 22. 40). And Paul said of the second part: "The whole law is fulfilled in one word, 'You

shall love your neighbour as yourself' " (Galatians 5. 14). The commandment to love God and one's neighbour sums up everything God wants
from us. God's basic requirements from Christians are *love, reconciliation,
justice* and *peace*. That will always be so. Without them you can't be a
Christian. Without them you aren't a Christian. Only if you can truth-
fully say that a Christian no longer has to worry about love, reconciliation, justice and peace, can you claim that morality has changed.

The Ten Commandments

But some people will say: That's too general, we have to be more precise.
That is true. And Scripture is more exact. There is a detailed code a "law"
which is "wholly" dependent on the double commandment of love of
God and our neighbour? It is the Ten Commandments. If we read through
them carefully, we see that the first three contain everything to do with
the love of God; and the next seven, whatever serves love, justice and
peace among men. As in the case of loving God and our neighbour, you
cannot be a Christian without the Ten Commandments. Following them
is essential if you want to "enter into life" (Matthew 19. 17).

But aren't the Ten Commandments far too general? Whoever really
loves, thinks justly, and is ready for peace and reconciliation, surely
doesn't have to have all the details of what he is to do and not to do?
For a true believer, being good and making the world a better place are
obvious duties. If he really believes, then the commandments – the
commandment of love and the Ten Commandments – have nothing new
to say to him. They only support and make plain what his faith knows if
it is really faith. Whoever has the commandments in his heart in faith,
knows in almost every case, without any long debate, what he has to do.
If he does debate with himself, there is a strong suspicion that conscience
is struggling with self-interest and looking for a way out. Here too morals
haven't changed, and mustn't change; it is man who has to change and
make his behaviour consistent with his faith.

New moral questions

That is true of most situations in our daily life. But some cases do seem
vague and ambiguous – those where something really has changed. We
have to ask and answer two questions here. First: How do we explain
that? Quite simply. The Church gets round to things. It takes time. We
gradually realize our mistakes and come to understand the real demands
of faith much better. In most cases where morality seems to have altered,
it is a case of general opinions having been confused with the demands
of faith, and the error being noticed eventually. Those harsh rules in the
area of the sixth commandment under which our grandparents and

parents were raised didn't derive from Christian belief but from a nineteenth-century sense of propriety we now consider merely "prudish". Since Christians are always children of their age, they looked on what was generally thought to be right at the time as commanded by God. That has often happened. It will happen again and again. In such cases change is no more than the dissolution of an illicit marriage of faith and the spirit of the age.

There is something much more important: "changes" in morals which come about when we have to face things which are wholly new and for which we have to find the right standards of moral behaviour. Who twenty years ago would have thought that behaviour in traffic could ever become a real moral question? Who would have thought that environmental pollution would have changed from a nuisance to a matter of the life and death of humanity in industrial areas, and therefore a very serious moral question? Who twenty years ago would have thought that political activity can be a Christian duty, and that voting isn't enough, if state organs are inadequate? How many realized that they couldn't leave the justice and humanity of social life to the State?

A Christian is bound in conscience to judge all social issues by Christian standards. But it is not always clear what that means. He has to find out the precise implications of God's commandments. Earlier standards that were quite valid at one time suddenly have to be jettisoned when circumstances change. Personal freedom, individual liberty, has been a supreme value for some time. To limit it seems almost blasphemous by the standards of ten years ago. But what if that freedom causes people to die on our roads, landscapes to be destroyed and cities to become inhuman hellscapes? Clearly very few of us would defend individualism: new problems and greater knowledge of the effects of unbridled liberty on health and natural or urban scenery have "changed" morality.

Necessary and arbitrary change

But how can we distinguish between necessary and arbitrary change in morality? We have to discover the facts first. Sometimes problems are so complicated that we can't find the necessary information by ourselves, but have to seek the help of experts.

When we have that information, the rest isn't so difficult, if we can suppress our own wishes and interests. For example we need only ask: What just claim has my fellow man — another driver or a pedestrian, someone living in an industrial area, a family which can't pay a high rent, and so on — on me, my love, my consideration, or my desire for peace and quiet? As a rule the right answer appears quickly. Then we must say: That is a commandment of God for me. That's what God wants of me. Not because it's written up or down somewhere, but because the

ten basic commandments of God, summarized in the twofold commandment of love for God and my neighbour, make it obvious.

Should Catholics be "left-wing"?

Even if Christians clearly have to choose what is just and loving when
new problems arise, the details of a just solution can be difficult, particularly in the political field. Often a clearly recognized moral principle
doesn't reveal the right solution in advance. It can happen — and the
second Vatican Council expressly stated this in its Constitution on the
Church in the modern world — that Christians who are united in faith
part company in their political views. It is wrong to think that Catholics
must all share the same political opinion. If Catholics choose political
options which some like to think of as "left-wing", that certainly doesn't
mean they aren't true Christians. If anyone thinks the opposite he has
to have very good, properly thought-out reasons and evidence for doing
so. The same is true when "left-wing" Christians declare that "non-left"
viewpoints mean their proponents are un-Christian.

Modern virtues

Whoever wants to live a Christian life has to concern himself with the
appropriate "virtues". "Virtue" is a word people don't very much like
these days. When they hear it they think of "obedience" — of attitudes
and behaviour which are inappropriate to a grown up man, because they
prevent him from responsibly deciding the course of his own life.

But virtue also means keeping to the right behaviour. Surely a
Christian has to concern himself with *modern* virtues which enable him
to act properly as a Christian when faced with the demands of our times?
A booklet that came out a few years ago listed the following "virtues":
responsibility, lack of prejudice, tolerance, love of peace, objectivity,
open-mindedness, respect, courage, collegiality (or deciding and acting
jointly), comradeship, discretion, restitution, sympathy, friendliness,
calmness, thankfulness, reliability, self-control, patience and readiness to
help.

When we read that list we think: Yes, that's how people should be.
That's what's demanded of Christian faith today. These "virtues of
modern man" are the present-day commandments of God. This is conduct
worth striving for; behaviour which is good and effective even without
faith. Christian "morals" hasn't got much that's unique about it — what
it has is a special ground or basis: the love of God which we have received
from him. Christians can and should work together with all men of good
will who are concerned for justice, and who struggle to bring about a
good, really human life in the modern world.

It is not a bad but a good sign when an insight into moral demands which Christians for a long time thought were peculiar to them, now extends far beyond the boundaries of the Church and even to men who want nothing to do with the Church.

When non-Christians surpass you and are quicker than Christians in doing the right thing to "change morals" remember that every iota of justice and peace achieved on this earth is a fragment of God's creation redeemed in reality. Why should God despise that achievement of non-Christians, to whom he is perhaps much closer than they think? And why shouldn't you learn from non-Christians?

9

What is sin?

People who talk about old-fashioned morals also tend to think of sin as an out-of-date Christian concept.

A matter of feeling?
But often Christians who are quite serious about living a life of faith speak of "sin" with mixed feelings. They use the term with some degree of irony, and can't really take it seriously. In the past much anxiety was stirred up by calling a whole range of things "sin" quite wrongly. And behind "sin" was the "hell" you would finish up in if you weren't sorry for sin and didn't go to confession. Today Christianity doesn't depend so much on fear. That is good. But with fear a certain sensitivity to sin has gone too.

Christian belief is not Christian if it refuses to recognize the reality of sin. Yet sin is not a matter of feeling. We are not denying the reality of sin if we say we don't "feel" it. The person most horrified by it hasn't the most profound understanding of what sin is. Someone who feels no horror of sin isn't necessarily without an awareness of it. Sin is a reality sensed only by faith. It doesn't depend on feeling. But what is sin?

Self-glorification
Faith recognizes God as the Lord of human life. God isn't Lord because he makes men slaves, but because he gives them life and invites them into his presence and into communion with him in the deepest sense, and asks men to find the whole joy and happiness of life in this way. Man senses this invitation, accepts it and lives in a way which corresponds to it – what we call "believing". Or he refuses it or renounces it, and that we call "sin". "Sinning" means saying no to God, refusing life with God.

Sin is the opposite of belief, of faith, and therefore cannot be recognized without faith.

But a man doesn't just say No. He can't just refuse. He does it because he sees an alternative. Because he says Yes to something else. This alternative to God can only be man himself. Whoever refuses faith wants to live not through God but through himself. The essence of sin is self-glorification.

It can be very direct. A man sees himself faced with the choice of believing or building on himself alone, of loving God or loving himself before all other things — and decides against God, for himself. The theology of earlier centuries spoke in such cases of "pride" or "arrogance", even of "hatred of God". Something like that is possible. We can't say it doesn't happen when an intelligent man reaches beyond his capabilities. On the other hand we can never judge by external appearance and say: This man is sinful, even when we think we can see clear signs of sin. Only God looks so closely into hearts that he really knows what is wrong with a man. But a No to God is seldom spoken so directly. In most cases a man says it indirectly, by behaving sinfully towards his fellow men.

Egotism

Sin towards one's fellow man is sin towards *God*. Sometimes we meet with the opinion that sin towards one's fellow man has nothing to do with God, but only with that fellow man — that restitution has to made only to him. That is wrong, if we remember the last two chapters. All duty in love and justice to our fellow men is based on the fact that we have previously received God's love in faith. The believer extends this love to others, or he does not really believe.

How can we remain with God, how can we continue to live in communion with God, if we don't extend his love to others? The logic of this is emphasized by the first letter of John: "If someone says, I love God, and hates his brother, he is a liar" (1 John 4. 20). All guilt towards men is not just guilt, but sin: in other words, it is directed not only against men but against God whose love we refuse to extend to others. It really doesn't make any difference whether we "feel" that or not.

If sin — direct or indirect — is self-glorification, one unmistakable feature enables us to recognize it in ourselves and perhaps in others: that is egotism, the demand what everything must ultimately revolve about oneself. In sinning a man makes himself a replacement god.

Original sin

This worship of the idols of self-glorification and egotism is very deep-set in men. Not only in our own lives, but as far back as we can go into human history, men have been driven by this desire for self-glorification. The Bible's pronouncements on the subject only support what the history of civilization show: men have always wanted to be absolute lords themselves. They even wanted to subject their gods to themselves. Somewhere at the beginning of human history too far back to reach, there must have been a start to this self-glorification – otherwise it is impossible to explain such a fateful tendency. Christian belief calls that beginning of self-glorification "original sin". Man comes into the world with this basic inclination to self-glorification, despite all personal decision and determination. And in his personal decision he will tend to yield to that inclination, all other things being equal. All sinful actions bring to the surface what is already within mankind.

Self-enslavement

Sin is self-enslavement. We often hear the opinion that without the courage to break through taught notions of morality, without the courage to "sin", a man would not become free, mature and self-responsible. There is some truth in that: as for instance when someone has wrongly persuaded another man that he is wholly encompassed by sin and can hardly go a step without sinning. But if we remember the real nature of sin, it is foolish to maintain that sin liberates. The opposite is true.

Belief makes man free in the deepest sense. It frees him from care for himself; it liberates him from the pressure of all kinds of precepts, on which salvation is supposed to depend. It gives him the one duty of love, and that is not coercion but self-understanding – for anyone who has understood the gift of God's love.

Whoever does not believe, whoever refuses God, cuts off his life from the source of true freedom. Then it all starts again: worry about yourself; the awful questions of the meaning of your own existence (for it soon becomes obvious that you don't give your own life that meaning); the expenditure of energy needed to get control of life. Everything is lost and pointless if you *don't* succeed in making something out of your transient life. There is no more energy left over for others, because you are primarily concerned with yourself. You are your real neighbour. Whoever will not depend on the true God, has to depend on himself alone. That has never led to any convincingly acceptable end.

Self-alienation

Self-alienation or estrangement is the second feature of sin. Whoever serves himself alone becomes a stranger to himself. He becomes the caricature of a man, a caricature of himself. For he is called to partake of the glorious freedom of the children of God (Romans 8. 12). If you refuse that call, how can you become anything other than a caricature of yourself? When you are faced with an absolute egotist, with an unreliable boss, with people who think only of money, with a power-hungry man in public life, who only uses men and friendship to get himself on, with an exploiter of the weak and defenceless — you say spontaneously: He's no longer human!

"Mortal" and "venial" sin

Sin seldom shows itself in a so to speak chemically pure state in a single, really evil action. Abandonment of God is usually a chain of sinful decisions, which individually are perhaps not so terrible. An absolute form of mortal sin is the unusual step of direct rejection of God; of radical pride and hatred of God. A sin is serious too if it is only indirectly directed against God himself, but seriously affects a fellow human, as in the case of murder — sin of that order of gravity is known traditionally as "mortal sin". "Venial sin" is an action which doesn't accord with God and his love, but is far from conscious separation from God, because it is either an insignificant matter or something which does not happen with the sinner's full consent and insight.

This distinction helps us to achieve a certain clarity of conscience. But it can be dangerous when misused to classify something as "venial". The distinction between mortal or "highly serious" and "venial" sin isn't made to quieten our conscience but to refine it. We should remember that it isn't the weighty sins which make our Christian life so unconvincing and ineffectual but the dusty layer of everyday minor instances of unloving behaviour and lost opportunities. Those are the things which cause people to say: What has Christian faith done for that man that's in any way special? The best thing for our conscience isn't to ask whether sins are mortal or venial, but to ask what demands, big and small, have been made of us, and to take quite seriously *any* refusal of those demands, irrespective of whether we think that rejection has separated us or not from God. There is also the slow death of faith brought about by the piling up of a number of "venial" sins. That happens when you constantly reject small claims on your love and care in everyday life. Eventually you no longer know or recognize what faith and a life of faith mean.

Modern sins

There are such things as sins of the age. There are "modern virtues", and offences against them are special sins of the times. Ask yourself what the areas are in which special moral responsibility is called for nowadays. The following come to mind at once: neighbourliness (sins of omission through a lack of concern for one's fellow men, perhaps in a big family, business or institution); business (say the unrestricted use of a trade advantage); traffic (careless flouting of traffic regulations, the endangering of others' lives); work ethics (the exploitation of modern social security for the sake of laziness); politics (standing aside from problems which can be solved only if everyone works at them); aid (a lack of readiness to give, when one's purse is concerned, even though others are without the minimum needed to exist).

Hell

And what about hell? There is a "hell". But it's just like heaven in not being a place which one could give a description of. Hell is that state of separation from God which is brought about by sin. Hell begins in sin itself, here on earth. A man's eyes are only really open to what self-glorification has brought him to when he won't give up sin and stays like that.

In all discussion of the connexion between sin and hell we have to take care. We cannot say about any man from observance of his external behaviour that he is really totally cut off from God, not even when he has persisted in that refusal right up to his last conscious moment. Therefore we cannot say of *any* man that he is "in hell" or "has gone to hell". Not even of people about whom all our sensitivity leads us to assume that that is the case: not of Judas, nor of Hitler, nor of Stalin; there is *no* case in which we can venture such an opinion. The Church has always taught that there is a hell, but it has never confirmed that any man has suffered that state. A modern theology professor has put it like this: "No one goes to hell who doesn't want to go there". That may seem surprising but it's true.

Nowadays we no longer inquire into sin as if we knew nothing of redemption. We inquire only into sins that God has basically forgiven. That is the only way in which we can fully come to terms with the reality of sin. Only out of the grace of God in Christ do we obtain insight into the existence of original sin (cf. Romans 5. 12-21). But God has accepted us as we are, with all our guilt, with all our failures. Ultimately we have nothing to fear in sin. We should simply remain with God, who always accepts us again, despite everything.

This fundamental truth of our faith once again throws a light on the question of hell. How can God begin again with a man who is so self-glorifying that he won't let his sin be forgiven? He would have to deprive him of his freedom in order to convert him. And that's something God won't do. God's respect for the freedom he has given mankind in spite of the risk of its misuse is the reason for the existence of the dark possibility we call "damnation" and "hell".

But God *has* forgiven. There are no complicated special things which have to be done in order to ward off God's punishment. We need only be always trusting and prepared to do what we read in the Gospel in the essence of the message of Jesus: "Repent and believe in the Gospel" (Mark 1. 15).

10

Do infants have to be baptized?

If you ask parents bringing their baby to be baptized what they think
happens in baptism they are liable to answer: He or she becomes a child
of God. If you ask if that means it was a child of the devil beforehand,
the same parents will of course say No! But that answer doesn't seem
logical, given the first one. Yet they are right. In the Letter to the
Ephesians we read: "In Christ he chose us before the world was founded,
to be dedicated, to be without blemish in his sight, to be full of love; and
he destined us . . . to be accepted as his sons through Jesus Christ, in order
that the glory of his gracious gift, so graciously bestowed on us in his
Beloved, might resound to his praise" (Eph 1. 4-6). No child comes into
the world "in the devil's clutches". From the beginning of his life every
child received has bestowed on him the glory of God's "gracious gift":
God's grace which marks him out as a child of God.

God's first word about life
Yet it is true to say that a child becomes a child of God through baptism.
How? Let us look at what happens and is said. There's no magic; now
that we hear it all in our own language any suspicion of that is absent.
There is the Church. the community of the faithful, embodied in the
parish or at least in the family and their friends who are bringing the child
to be baptized. This Church looks at the life of a man who has just been
born or has already reached adulthood. In the name of God and through
the person administering baptism (a priest or deacon or in a case of
necessity any willing Christian) the Church has something to say about
this life: the most fundamental and all-inclusive thing that can be said
about a human life: "Have you forgotten that when we were baptized
into union with Christ Jesus we were baptized into his death? By baptism
we were buried with him, and lay dead, in order that, as Christ was raised
from the dead in the splendour of the Father, so also we might set our

feet upon the new path of life" (Rom. 6. 3-8). That is how Paul puts it. Other words that we find in the Bible or which occur in the baptismal service say the same thing from other viewpoints· This man is a "child of God", a "temple of the Holy Spirit".

The candidate for baptism comes into contact with what brought Jesus Christ into the world. His life is placed under the sign of the death and resurrection of Jesus. It is a life directed towards death — like Jesus's life. But this death sets no limit to the power of the living God. The life of the baptized person is intended to be *only* life and a *fulfilled* life, despite death.

What pronouncement on human life could be more important and wide-ranging than· that it should be *really* life and not just waiting over the years for death? And that is the statement the Church makes about the candidate for baptism, adding: You are free from the power of sin. Sin is forgiven you, personal sin just as much as supra-personal sin, into which man is born and which we call "original sin". Sin means death, because it cuts us off from the source of life, from God. Man cannot live and at the same. time be in sin. Therefore baptism must liberate us from sin, or it could not be what it is.

Baptism and belief

Of course what is said in baptism doesn't work of its own accord. It has to be accepted, wanted with the heart and spirit, proven; it must so sharpen and enliven the spirit and the mind that they look at life in an entirely new way. It should be the beginning of an entirely new way of living and behaving. In short it has to be *believed*. Therefore baptism makes the baptized person a member of the Church. For the Church is the community of those who have received the word of life in faith. Whoever receives it anew is necessarily confirmed as a member of that community. Whoever believes belongs to the faithful. Therefore baptism also has so to speak a *legal* effect. It makes the baptized person a member of the community of the Church with all the rights and duties which apply in that Church.

It could seem possible for baptism to consist only of an exchange of proclamation and confession of faith. It could be restricted to a written document regarding church membership. But it isn't human to do such important things in such a dull and routine manner. Since the earliest days the Church has celebrated this "exchange of words" and this reception into the community in the form of a meaningful action. An element is used whose significance, whose symbolism, is understood by men of all cultures and civilizations: water. Its depth and flow illustrate the process of descending, of death with Christ. Its freshness represents the new life with the resurrected Christ. Its purity represents liberation from guilt. The words spoken at the point of baptism summarize what baptism has to say about human life: "In the name of the Father" — who has made us and stands at the beginning of this human life — "and of the Son" — who though his suffering and death gives us back life itself — "and of the Holy Spirit" — who unites us in faith and love with God and with one another. That is what the Church learned from Jesus.

Infant baptism

Should we baptize infants? Is there any meaning in publicly pronouncing over a human life virtually at its beginning words about death and resurrection with Christ? Certainly, or at least there's no imperative objection against doing so. Is it appropriate to say at so early a stage that this life is no longer held in the dark night of sin and therefore that it need not lose the life given it by God? We can't stop that being said. Can we make a babe in arms a member of a community? Of course we can. By his birth he becomes a member of civil society and already has rights which no one can deny him. But of course a child can't say his own Yes to all that. He can't make a personal acceptance yet. Therefore infant baptism is only meaningful when it is certain that the child will grow up in a Christian family, which will show him the ways to personal faith in an adequate form. Personal preparation for baptism, which even today is required of any adult candidate, takes the form of Christian education in infant baptism.

Of course it's possible to give a Christian education with a view to baptism later on. Therefore children *don't have to be* baptized as infants. Whether infant baptism really gives a life of faith, whether it isn't in a sense wasted, can only be shown when the growing man can confront the message of the Gospel in the freedom of his heart. The man baptized as a child has no advantage over a new convert in so to speak missionary territory. But in a Christian family children *should* be baptized. It is no danger to freedom or belief. A Christian education would no longer deserve the name if it were merely a form of training in belief. Instead it must show the growing individual, according to each stage of growth, what faith is as something which only he can decide on personally, and which no one else can decide for him. If it works like that, then it is not restricting but helpful if baptism has already taken place. Men aren't usually so keen on making clear-cut decisions. A peaceful growing up into a decision which does not remove the freedom to reject, is usually to be preferred to the kind of decision which can too easily be made for transient reasons.

God's love

But there is another important reason. Infant baptism brings out more clearly than adult baptism that God has loved us from the start and given us his grace from the start. And that all our faith and readiness for baptism do not *deserve* it. A baby can't prepare for baptism. Since we bring it for baptism, we acknowledge and show publicly that God's grace always comes first in our entire life: not the reward for our work, but the gift that can't be earned, that gives our life support and direction from the start. Therefore, it is best if Christian families (as has been the custom in the Church for centuries) bring their children for baptism *soon* after birth. It is also good if — contrary to past practice — parents wait a time, and postpone the ceremony to a suitable day when the whole family and especially the mother can be there. Infant baptism is a Christian family's celebration of faith.

11

Why should we go to church on Sunday?

It is a commandment of the Church that every Catholic Christian should go to Mass on Sundays and holidays of obligation. We are also told that we are guilty before God if we miss our Sunday duty without good cause. What is the point of this commandment? Why does the Church take away the only morning in the week which is peaceful? Can't we pray just as easily at home?

"Leisure time"

When preparing for a synod of bishops a few years ago, the German Church circulated a questionnaire among German Catholics, asking why and with what expectations people went to church on Sunday. The following was the result: Far from all Catholics go to Mass on Sunday on average 30 per cent at the most. Well over half of those go because they find peace for prayer and hope in the possibility of meeting God, Jesus Christ. For in the week, in the rush and tumble of everyday working and home life there is little or no time for prayer. The churchgoer doesn't seem to find that the Church is robbing him of his peace, but on the contrary, that the Church puts a little pressure on because it knows that churchgoing is good for his faith and Christian life.

If we ask: Why should we go to church on Sunday? then the first answer would seem to be: Because we need a kind of "leisure time" for our faith. We have hardly any peace in the week because we have wo much to think about and so much to do. As Christians we must take care that all that happens then is done out of faith and never hurts love. But our faith is so preoccupied with just living that it has hardly the time or the strength to take a look at itself, and that means at what God has done to us and is still doing. Therefore our faith needs a rest, just as our energies generally need time to recoup. Sunday churchgoing is a rest for faith. It can and should be so anyway. For we can get a release from the rigours and constraints of everyday duties. We meet people with the same faith. We don't have to explain anything to anyone. In prayer, reading, preaching and celebrations we become newly aware of what our faith means to us, how we are joined to God through Jesus Christ, what we may hope from God and what effect that will have on our lives. Just as a family celebration, if properly arranged and carried out, can loosen things up and give new energy for working days after the celebration, so Sunday Mass — when properly arranged and celebrated — can give our faith strength for the tasks of the week to come.

Celebration

What happens at Sunday Mass? Prayer, readings and a sermon provide the framework for a celebration whose highpoint is a common eating and drinking. If you took someone who had never heard anything about Christian belief to a Sunday Mass and asked him afterwards what he would call the whole thing, the answer would be eating and drinking with a preparation. Perhaps he wouldn't call it a "meal", for we don't sit down at a table with places and dishes in front of us; there are far too many people present. But perhaps he would compare what he'd seen with a "reception", as for example for a Silver Wedding or some anniversary a lot of people are invited to celebrate. No one there seems to know everyone else, but at least everyone knows at least a few people. They stand or sit together, and talk about the event which has prompted the reception. Someone makes a speech of welcome and thanks, refreshments are given out; something small to eat and drink, not in order to feed the guests fully as at a meal, but in order to create a festive, communual atmosphere. It is an old experience that nothing joins men so firmly together as eating and drinking together.

Jesus's "Last Supper"

This comparison with a "reception" helps us to understand the Mass better in the form we know it today. It suits my remark that the Mass is a kind of rest or leisure time for the celebration of faith. But if we had to find the right kind of form for a leisure-time recreation of faith, would we think of a reception or something like it, and would we organize it as the Mass is organized today? Not really. What is special about the Mass and why does it take precisely this form? The decisive reason for the Mass being as it is is that Jesus himself introduced it, not in all the details of the form we know, but in its essentials. The celebration which is known as the Eucharist or Mass today goes back to the celebration which Jesus held with his followers the day before his Passion and which we therefore call the Last Supper. Some Protestants still call their Eucharist the Lord's Supper for that reason. The Eucharist is the repetition of the Last

Supper, in accordance with the injunction issued by Jesus to his disciples at the meal: "Do this in memory of me."

There are four reports of the Last Supper in the New Testament (Matthew 26. 17-29; Mark 14. 12-25; Luke 22. 7-23; 1 Corinthians 11. 23-29). They don't accord word for word, because each reporter mixes his own concerns and viewpoints with the description. But they agree in essentials. There are three things to look out for.

1. Jesus chooses the form of the Jewish Easter meal. This paschal feast was a form of divine service. Eating and drinking were set in a framework similar to that of our Eucharist: prayers, songs, readings, a speech from the person presiding over the meal. The theme of the meal was the great deeds God made manifest to his people, above all their liveration from slavery in Egypt. They wanted to recall that at every Easter meal and to thank God for it.

2. The paschal meal recalled the ancient agreement of God with the people of Israel. But Jesus speaks of a new agreement or covenant which replaces the old one. Jesus says that this new covenant is made in his blood. In the Last Supper Jesus "unbloodily" anticipates his death. The feast which the disciples celebrate now takes them into the new agreement with God which Jesus establishes by his self-abandonment to death. *After* Jesus's death and resurrection the anticipation becomes the *memory.* Therefore every celebration of the Eucharist places the participant in the new covenant with God confirmed by Jesus, which was what happened to Jesus's disciples in the room where the Last Supper was celebrated.

Sacrifice of the new covenant

3. During the old Easter meal people ate a roast lamb in memory of the exodus from Egypt. Jesus replaced it with bread and wine and said something very mysterious about them: "This is my body which will be given up for you" . . . "This is the cup of my blood . . . shed for you and for all men". At first these words tell us again that Jesus's going to his death is present in this celebration and that his sacrifice is made for the Father in heaven and for men. Therefore the Eucharist has been known for a long time as the "sacrifice of the new covenant". For the sacrifice of the paschal lamb is replaced now by Jesus's self-surrender to God on behalf of men. Unlike the ancient sacrifices, however, Jesus's sacrifice is once and for all. Therefore the Eucharist is not a new sacrifice and not a repetition of the sacrifice on the cross, but the representation, the realization or making present now, of Jesus's unique death on the cross. As the sacrifice of the new covenant, that replaced the paschal lamb and all sacrifices of the old Covenant.

Presence of Christ

But Jesus's statement is mysterious in another sense. Jesus equated himself with the offerings which he gave to the disciples and told them to give in his memory. For "This is my body — this is my blood" means "This is me". How are we to understand that? In the history of the Church there have been many attempts to explain Jesus's words. No one person can wholly elucidate the mystery of these words. But I can try to show a direction in which it is possible to understand the equation of Jesus with the offerings or, as we say, Christ's presence in the bread and wine.

One thing is clear: there is no question of magic of any kind. The bread and the wine do not change outwardly into Jesus's body and blood, nor is Jesus present in his earthly form in the bread and wine. In their external form, shape, colour, taste and ingredients, the bread and wine are the *sign* of Christ's presence. But how can a person equate himself with the sign, something that signifies his presence? Think of a husband who gives his wife a couple of dozen roses every year on their wedding anniversary, just as he did when they were married. What does that mean? The man is saying to his wife: Look, these roses express the same love with which I married you. These roses are my devotion to you, today as then. This comparison brings us closer to understanding what Jesus means. Jesus isn't present materially. He is *personally* present, invisible but nonetheless real. He is present through his love and this love is the same as the love which brought him to die for us, and is expressed in the same gifts as those he gave at the Last Supper.

Only one thing is different about the roses, and this is where imagination runs into difficulties. Even the most expressive sign men can concieve can't remove the difference between the sign and the one who gives it. The roses aren't the man. Indeed the man could pretend. He could cheat with the roses, for human signs are never wholly trustworthy. But Jesus's signs are quite reliable. Hypocrisy is excluded. Because he no longer shares our life in space and time he can cancel the distinction between sign and person. He can put his whole reality invisibly into the sign of his devotion. That is something we cannot comprehend but only believe through Jesus's word, and in that belief we rejoice in his closeness to us.

The presence of Christ, who died for us and was raised up by God, is the nearness of God himself, which makes a life whole. Therefore our whole faith comes together in the Eucharist: We hear the good news (readings), learn its application to our lives (sermon or homily), celebrate the memory of those events in which God came irrevocably close to us, in other words the death and resurrection of Jesus, experience his presence in receiving the bread and wine, and recall the consequences for our lives . . . Therefore the liturgical constitution of the liturgy of the second Vatican Council calls the Eucharist the high point towards which all the Church's activity is directed and at the same time the source from which all its strength flows. Nowhere in the action of the Church and in Christian life is our entire faith summarized like that. Nowhere can faith reflect on itself in so concentrated a manner as in the Eucharist.

Concelebrating the Eucharist

We don't go to Mass like forced labourers. We should be daring enough to behave as if we were at a good friend's with whom we don't have to put on airs and behave quite so formally. We can greet our friends peacefully, exchange a few words outside or inside the church. We don't need to "prepare" ourselves for Mass. It has its own preparatory section: song of entry, confession of guilt and prayer. It is a matter of "breathing" our faith; everyday affairs and worries should be left outside. We should listen to the readings as we should to any good and interesting news item: with curiosity rather than "devotionally", attentively, listening for the details, especially when we know the texts already. Hymns or silences between readings are intended to indicate our Yes to God's word. Application to our lives is the preacher's work. Therefore we should be just as eager to hear what he has to say as in the case of the reading. But this time it is critical curiosity that we must show. The basic question is always: Does this sermon really concern *my* life, or is he right off the track? Only if you encounter a sermon c..itically — at first silently but later in discussion with your family and the preacher — is a sermon really working as it should. Confession of faith or creed and bidding prayers are a twofold answer to what has been heard: Yes to God's presence among men which gives us the courage to talk to him on behalf of ourselves and others.

After the preparation of offerings (which we should watch) the real heart of the Eucharist starts. Here we should listen to and pray with and search out everything we know to be the essence of the Eucharist. Going to communion should be a normal part of the Eucharist. Sometimes many churchgoers seem to stay away from communion for reasons which really aren't valid. And communion should do what it signifies: community, peace. At the end of Mass, when it is over, but really as part of it, there should be announcements with practical references to the life of the community and its tasks.

The peaceful communual atmosphere should continue after the Eucharist. It's not a good idea to rush off as quickly as possible. You can talk, go home together, discuss something with the preacher, go for coffee with some friends. If the Mass is experienced as peaceful community, then it won't seem a burden which has to be imposed by rule.

Sunday duty

But what if it is a nuisance? Well, it isn't a bad thing to put a little pressure on ourselves, or else the "weakness of the flesh" would soon win the day. There is no need to be afraid of hellfire, of course, if you stay at home for good reasons that your grandparents wouldn't have thought good. But often the limit between bad and good is difficult to draw. It is a good idea to make it your duty to go regularly to Sunday Mass; even if you don't feel particularly in the "mood" you can always give thanks. And thanks is only another name for the whole celebration — the Mass or Eucharist.

12

Do we need to be confirmed?

Should we accept a bunch of flowers when someone offers it to us? We don't have to take it; but it would be rather odd if we didn't. We don't have to be confirmed in order to be in God's community, but it would be strange if we weren't.

Baptism and confirmation

Confirmation doesn't stand at the centre of church life and the individual Christian's life like baptism and the Eucharist. The Bible doesn't speak half so clearly about what we now call confirmation as it does about baptism and the Lord's Supper (see Acts 8. 12-17; 19. 1-7). Confirmation also seems rather complicated. The Bishop usually administers it, and since that isn't possible very often, candidates come together in relatively large numbers for what can be a rather exhausting event.

Yet there are good grounds for keeping confirmation. In the midst of the congregation the community the bishop lays his hands on the candidate, signs a cross on his head with oil (in accordance with very ancient practice), and says: "I sign you with the sign of the cross and I confirm you with the chrism of salvation, in the name of the Father, and of the Son, and of the Holy Spirit". The process is rather like baptism. Instead of water there's oil, and instead of "I Baptize . . ." there is "I sign you. . . and confirm you . . ." Is confirmation just a sort of repetition of baptism? Something superfluous if we take baptism seriously?

Confirmation is certainly the "second part" of baptism. In the early Church confirmation was often administered right after baptism – even to infants – and of course it's only given once. And there is the long tradition that confirmation has something to do with the faith of a grown man. It is directed to mature faith. It is intended to strengthen that faith. We can see the meaning of confirmation when we look at the difference between a faith which has just begun – as expressed in baptism – and a mature faith.

Mature faith

The more a Christian grows into his faith, the more he discovers that he must defend and show forth his faith in new and unexpected circumstances. His faith is often exposed to open and hidden persecution. On the other hand his faith isn't just a private matter. To all men a Christian is a witness to the Word and to Christian life. But he discovers that his own strength of faith is limited and sometimes that it seems to be exhausted. Faith seems to keep behind what's expected of it. Life in faith becomes joyless and a routine affair. Nothing shines onto other people. Attacks weaken one. Compromises are made. The way of least resistance is chosen. "Mission to the world" becomes fine words which no longer describe an everyday reality.

If that is the case, persistence and a missionary dynamism are needed: a mature, realistic faith which is active in a missionary way. This is where confirmation comes in. As in baptism, the Church speaks in God's and Jesus's name, and makes a statement of faith about a man's life: It is as it were an explanation of the absolutely fundamental word of faith which baptism said about that man's life: Faith can manage this persistance, this strength of character, this missionary dynamism. The Church can say that on the basis of its experience of the strength God has given to faith. By the word and sign of the Church, confirmation is the acknowledgment of God that true strength of faith will not be failing in man. Whoever receives confirmation trusts in that. He promises to persist and to bear active witness. And therefore the Church as it were re-accepts him into the community of mature Christians. That is all the more meaningful since we are usually baptized as children when we are personally incapable of making a genuine decision of faith.

Life

That is not our work. Strength of faith and missionary daring are gifts of God, who gave us faith. Therefore confirmation is especially bound up with the name of the Holy Spirit. The Spirit who enables us to believe, gives that belief his strength and dynamic energy.

Now we have to live out of confirmation. We convert the faith of baptism into the strength of confirmation in our lives. The Bible speaks of the "fruits of the Spirit". What are they? Not a transient fascination but true persistence of faith accepting the burden of life in hope of the resurrection. Not superficial optimism but deep trust that God is always and everywhere close to us. Not unthinking carelessness, but firm confidence that God gives his meaning to our contribution to the world. Confirmation is for helping our fellow man, for resistance, for courage to go out and take responsibility wherever man's destiny is at stake, from education and work to politics. The confirmed man or woman can do all that if only he takes his confirmation seriously.

What age?
The age of confirmation has changed considerably in the Church's history. It is difficult to prove that it should be administered at any one age. But if it has to do with standing up to tests of faith, then a Christian receiving confirmation should already have experienced something of that testing and of the duty of witnessing to belief even in a difficult situation. He should therefore be past the age at which he is still living naively in the faith of others without having to decide for himself. Otherwise confirmation would be no more than a slightly different form of infant baptism. Surely the age at which a lot of people leave school is right — from fourteen to sixteen, depending on the country or locality. From that time onwards a young person sees clearly that his faith has grown out of its first shoes, and that it has to prove itself. That is a good time for the Church to tell him in God's name that he is receiving strength from the Holy Spirit.

13

Do we have to go to confession?

"I won't have private confession taken away by anyone. I wouldn't give it up for the whole world. I know what strength it has given me". Martin Luther praised confession thus. He didn't ask whether he had to go to confession; he was very happy to do so.

Public conversion

The question can be answered directly: No, you don't! In 1551, at Trent, the Church expressly declared that it was necessary to confess *grave sins* to a priest. With the exception of the case in which a Christian has fallen into grave sin — and this exception is no rule — no Christian has to confess at any time in his life. When the priest reminds us of the Church's commandment at the beginning of the Easter period, and says that all Catholics are duty-bound to receive the sacraments at Easter, only Easter communion is really intended. Confession is included only for the cases in which one is aware of grave sin.

It's another question whether we ought to confess. We have to watch out for two things: that our conversion remains serious and that the Church's creed stays clear. Conversion is given with faith itself. Mark summarizes all Jesus's teaching in the double injunction: "Be converted and believe in the Gospel" (Mark 1. 15). Conversion is to turn away from everything in our life which contradicts faith in God's closeness to us — in thought and action.

This conversion can be reversed — by some grave denial of faith and in life, but also by a whole chain of small inadequacies and omissions: by serious and "venial" sins. None of us is free from the second type. And so we have to do something so that we do not openly or unconsciously reverse our conversion to God in faith.

Faith makes us new men. If all Christians gave a bad or only average example of the new life in faith, other people would be quite justified in saying that was the fault of their faith? We have to do something to prevent our lapse or inadequacy from being attributed to faith. We have to make sure that people can distinguish faith from our own life.

There is no doubt that God will always forgive us our new failure, if we turn to him again, just as he forgave us when we were converted for the first time. It would seem to be enough to ask God for forgiveness on our own, in our room. But surely the seriousness of our conversion would be strengthened if it caused us a little more trouble that that. The conversion to which God has given his approval should take place publicly, for it relates to the Church. We are all human and tend to read what goes on inside from what happens outside. And we let what goes on outside affect the state of things within. Only if we decide not to turn back "on our own", but have the courage to do it clearly and memorably can we strengthen our determination not to do so easily again. If we are brave enough to accuse ourselves openly then we can ask others not to blame our faith for our failure.

Private confession

The public form in which we can and should show our conversion after *grave* failures is "auricular" confession before a priest. In the early centuries of Christianity public confession of sins was its equivalent. Relying on the Bible (Matthew 16. 18; 18. 18; John 20. 22-23) the Church distanced itself drastically from the sinner. He had to take a special place in church, dress appropriately, ask others to intercede for him, pray a lot, fast, be continent in marriage, often take no care of his person, and if he did that for weeks, months, even years, he was received back in the Church as a full member in a public service of reconciliation. This was intended to make clear to the congregation that the Church took sin seriously and would not allow the preaching of the gospel to be held in disrespect or contempt because of it.

"Auricular" confession alone, which developed in its present day form from the early Middle Ages, is a simpler process. You acknowledge or confess your sins to a priest (who has to keep quiet about them). The priest can discuss the sins with the penitent. At the end the priest tells the penitent in God's name that he is forgiven and reconciled. If the shame of confession seems too much for some people, they are possibly out for forgiveness and conversion at the least cost to themselves and don't really understand the gravity of what they've done. That seems typical of many modern people who boast of their ability to recognize their own guilt but whose confidence evaporates when they have to take a little trouble over their stance. And despite the simplicity and the "private" nature of confession, its public character is assured. The church doors are open at confession times. Everyone can see whoever is waiting for his or her turn in the confessional. If the managing director, the school child, the old woman who keeps that stall in the market, and the theology professor, are all in the same boat, all subject to the same public acknowledgment of sinfulness, it is clear enough that the Church doesn't tolerate sin because it can't tolerate something that contradicts what it preaches.

Examination of conscience

Small sins can be confessed at the same time as the really serious ones. But there is the danger of a regular trotting out of exactly the same list of minor inadequacies and not an occasion for a recognisably new beginning, obvious progress in the struggle against sin. Do we *have to* go to confession?

Since Vatican II increasing use has been made of communual confession or confessional services. All that is left of the usual process is the personal acknowledgment of sins and the private conversation with the confessor and a personally imparted absolution. Because that is only necessary in the case of grave sins, and because a general examination of conscience, a homily from the priest, and a general confession can be just as effective as "private" confession, venial sins can be submitted to God's judgment and mercy in a general confession which, within its obvious limitations, is a way to reconciliation with God and with the Church. Perhaps the Church everywhere will recognize it as a second form of the one sacrament of penance.

A general confession should make an examination of conscience less of a routine affair. Then private confession can be a more serious matter and the confessor can have more time for a more effective discussion of what is wrong with a penitent.

First things first

Any suspicion of routine or automatic confession must be ruthlessly excluded. Anyone tempted to frequent confession of a string of the same small sins should go less often to confession but take time instead over an examination of conscience that goes deeper than the usual run through the list of sins in a prayer book. Some very experienced confessors now answer the question: How often should I go to confession? with: Once or twice a year.

Everyone has the right to look for a confessor whom he can trust. No one is bound to go to the same one all the time. Especially when a priest gets angry or annoyed with a penitent, asks too much of him in penance, and so on. Then the penitent should avoid that confessor or even cut short the confession. The confessor can fail in his duty — unfortunately it still happens. He has to awaken the penitent's conscience if it needs awakening. He has to advise him and to help him reach a judgment of his own behaviour, and in that sense "direct" him. But the priest must never sit in judgment on the penitent.

The penitent has to give the priest an opportunity to talk to him meaningfully. Therefore his examination of conscience often has to go beyond the mere list of sins in a devotional book. Someone with a living faith will ask quite different questions about his own way of life to those in the average pious manual. He will look out more than for the typical modern sins which correspond to the typical demands that modern life makes of faith.

No confessor is omniscient, and entering the confessional won't make him so. Questions that experts in the Church can't agree on aren't likely to be easily solved in the confessional. Any confessor who puts his own opinion forward as the only valid one deserves suspicion. Good confessors can listen and are prepared to discuss things with their penitents. A penitent should always have the courage to argue back if what the confessor says isn't convincing.

Whether you like a confessional or a study or some other room for confession is a matter of personal preference. Some people like a discreet anonymous confessional, in spite of the discomfort. Others prefer a straightforward chat with the priest, especially when they have a difficult problem to discuss. The Church allows both possibilities. But if you want to talk something over in greater detail, it's fair to avoid the major festivals when priests are besieged by people.

A final tip. If you're hard of hearing don't make your confession with the crowd, but use the special confessional (if there is one), or make a private appointment for confession. Otherwise you will force the priest to speak loudly and you will probably speak too loudly yourself. If people roundabout can hear both of you, then the secrecy of the confessional and your own peace of mind are threatened.

14

What does the Church have to do with marriage?

What is a sacrament?

In the first centuries of Christianity, there was no common name for the special services of the Church. When a name was found, it was centuries before it was quite clear what the general idea of a sacrament really was. But even today that seems to be clear only to theologians. It is very difficult for an ordinary Christian to define a sacrament.

When discussing the individual sacraments I've avoided the word in the hope that an attentive reader will begin to glean some of its common features. All the "sacraments" I've mentioned until now are services, church services, and not private devotions of a group of people. Therefore since the earliest days, all over the world, they have taken the same basic shape. These services go back to the sacred action of God in Jesus, and to some extent the Bible reports their commencement or institution by Jesus himself. They present in words and visually comprehensible actions the Church's mission to the individual in the Church: and the individual answers them with a confession or acknowledgment of faith in "receiving" the sacrament.

The Catholic Church says that there are seven such sacraments or basic services, whereas most Protestant Churches (though not the Orthodox Church or the Anglican or Episcopalian Church) recognize only two sacraments: baptism and the Eucharist. But they do have services which correspond to the other sacraments of the Catholic Church. They take them very seriously even though they are not called sacraments.

The reasons for that need more than a book. Everything that the Catholic Church understands under the title "sacrament" allows for considerable differences despite the common term. That is especially true in the case of the ancient Catholic teaching that marriage is one of the seven sacraments. The word "sacrament" doesn't help us much here so it is best to ask: What does the Church have to do with marriage?

God's word on marriage

One thing is certain. Just as the Church has the general task of announcing God's word, it has to announce God's word on the union of men and women. God created human beings as men and women, blessed their union and made it fruitful. It is God's will that men and women who are married to one another should remain together all the days of their life. Despite several relaxations of this rule that had crept in in the course of time, Jesus re-emphasized the will of God in this respect. He put marriage on an entirely new footing, that of faith in the presence of God which he announced and brought to man. Married Christians stay together not because it's "rational", because they feel emotionally tied, or because it's necessary on account of the children. They stay together because they build on God's undying love as the basis of their own love and imitate that love in their marriage. All that is something that man cannot pronounce himself on the basis of his own reason. It has *to be said* to him. The Church, whose task it is to tell men what God has to say, has that much at least to do with marriage.

Church weddings

If marriage is evidence of the belief of the Church in the love of God then the Church must be interested in who is and who isn't married. Otherwise this particular witness to faith wouldn't be perfectly clear. There must be a church order of marriage.

Since the earliest times, the Church has celebrated marriages, witnessing and blessing the union between two Christians, so that, as St Ignatius, Bishop of Antioch at the beginning of the second century AD put it, the union is "made in the Lord". The external form of church marriage has varied considerably over the centuries. The present form in which the couple declare before a priest (usually the bride's priest) and two witnesses that they wish to marry, have their declaration of marriage confirmed by the Church and therefore count as married in the sight of the Church, developed in its essentials over 900 years ago. There were good reasons for that at the time. For example, state and society couldn't guarantee the freedom of marriage. The marriage partner wasn't chosen but ordained by the family. Women were often kidnapped for marriage purposes. Therefore the Church introduced the questions of free decision on marriage into the ecclesiastical betrothal that we know today. There are many good reasons for a church marriage today too. The State can guarantee the freedom of marriage today. But if the Church is to remain true to the word of God it cannot possibly recognize everything that the State has to do nowadays in regard to marriage, since the State takes neutral position in relation to the different religions and attitudes to life of its citizens.

Marriage as a sacrament

Nevertheless church marriage could take a different form. After all the Church has always recognized marriage without a priest when one just wasn't obtainable. For the last few years (though the rule differs from area to area) the Catholic Church has also agreed to allow Catholics to marry before a Protestant minister or registrar (a state official if the reasons are serious enough, though they have to be discussed with a priest first). It is not the actual betrothal in church that constitutes the sacrament of marriage, but married life supported by the grace of God. If the ecclesiastical celebration of marriage were the actual sacrament, there could be no exceptions. You can't baptize without water and you can't celebrate a Eucharist without bread and wine. But there are cases where a marriage recognized by the Church can take place without a priest. It is life in marriage that is important. Married life is like pouring water in baptism and the reception of holy communion in the Eucharist. Married life itself is the "service" and the "external action". There is hardly any witness to faith which is as powerful as a really successful marriage — which is not the same in any way as a marriage without any tension or conflict, and certainly not marriage as portrayed in cheap magazine stories and films. A marriage and a family which hold together in faith, and overcome their crises in love, is the best image of the unceasing love of God for man — and that is exactly what is meant by calling marriage a "sacrament".

Divorce?

A really Christian marriage is unbreakable. It is indissoluble because of the nature of the thing — because of what it is deep down. External laws of the Church only serve to support the real thing. If two baptized Christians who were fully conscious of what they were doing contracted a marriage in complete freedom the Church *could not* dissolve that marriage, if it wanted to. It can dissolve marriages as little as it can undo baptisms. If the Church allowed divorce that would mean that it no longer believed that God's love could make the love between two human beings last for ever.

But of course a lot of deception and self-deception can enter into a marriage. A couple can deceive the priest or the church authorities about the firmness of their intention to contract an unbreakable Christian marriage. They can make all sorts of reservations but say nothing to the priest, and so on. If that comes out later and it can be proved, then a marriage of that kind was not really a marriage (even though it seemed to be valid), but null and void and not a marriage as Christians understand it. A declaration of nullity means that the Church admits that it was deceived when it said the couple were married. Then of course the couple can marry again, even in a church, as long as they truly mean and are capable of meaning what they say and do.

People can also get married with good will and in full knowledge and acknowledgment of their duties, and afterwards it becomes clear, years later, that it was a mistake: that they deceived not the Church but themselves when they thought they could belong together in marriage. Today we know that self-deceptions of this kind can often arise from hidden psychological faults and immaturities which only come to the surface long after the marriage has taken place. Then people are faced with the ruin of a marriage which they had built their whole lives on. What is to be done in such cases?

Divorced people in the Church

For a long time the Church has been quite unyielding in these cases. If the marriage can't be shown to be null and void in the above sense, the Church treats such unsuccessful and broken marriages as valid. It does that so that the undissolubility of marriage won't be cast in doubt. If these unlucky married couples get a state divorce and remarry, the Church officially forbids them the sacraments, even if the new marriages are humanly successful and even if the children's religious education is irreproachable. But the Church doesn't exclude these Christians from the Church, as is sometimes wrongly claimed.

Nowadays people think this attitude is unmerciful. If you think of God's merciful attitude to men, and Jesus's behaviour towards sinners who turned from their sin, then it's hard to believe that God would be as tough as the Church still seems to be on people who have failed in a first attempt at marriage, have realized their self-deception and guilt, and have entered into a new marriage because they simply aren't made to live alone.

We can only hope that the Church will return to a less harsh practice of the kind it allowed in the first centuries of its existence, by not remarrying divorced people but allowing them to go to the sacraments after remarrying with a state ceremony. Of course the Church will still have to make clear in some other way that as far as Christians are concerned, marriage can never be a contract to be renounced at will, whatever we wish.

15

Why anoint the sick?

The letter of James speaks like no other part of the New Testament about everyday Christian life. It should be read right through at a sitting. It is not surprising that such a homely epistle should have something to say about Christians and sickness. James writes: "Is any one among you sick? Let him call for the elders of the church, and let them pray over him, anointing him with oil in the name (that is, the power) of the Lord (Jesus); and the prayer of faith will save the sick man, and the Lord will raise him up; and if he has committed sins, he will be forgiven" (James 5. 14-5).

This text is the basis of the sacrament that we now know as the anointing of the sick. The priest comes to the sick person, anoints him or her with blessed oil on the forehead and on the hands, and prays that by this holy anointing and his gracious mercy God may give the sick man the grace of the Holy Spirit. This prayer and the text from the letter of James show that the anointing isn't there only for the dying but for all those who are seriously ill. We used to call this sacrament Extreme Unction or the Last Anointing, which ignored its more general application.

In January 1973 Pope Paul VI stressed this aspect of the sacrament, which is clear from the use of oil, which was a medicine in ancient times, and therefore served to *heal* the sick person. But the anointing isn't carried out for every little common cold but in illnesses where the patient is in danger of death, in serious car accidents and so on. It can and should be repeated in the case of another illness or a long-lasting illness growing worse.

Like confirmation, the anointing of the sick belongs with baptism. It re-emphasizes in a special way what God says in baptism about the whole course of life. A man *wants to* live and learns that he *has to* die. Here baptismal faith is brought right up against it. Now you look death in the face and can't put things off any more. Will you face death with Jesus and hope in the resurrection as you promised in baptism?

In this hour the Church, represented by your family, perhaps by good friends and acquaintances and the priest, stands at your bedside, and in the name of Jesus tells the sick person in words and action to trust in God. He raised Jesus from the dead and will not let you be vanquished by death. The sick person hears these words and in receiving the anointing and praying acknowledges his belief and accepts his future destiny as God decides. If he gets well he thanks God for his recovery. If he dies then he knows that his guilt has been forgiven him just as God always forgave him during his lifetime. Here too we find all the things which make up a "sacrament".

Fear of the anointing

It is hard to see why so many Christians are afraid of the anointing of the sick. Sometimes they seem to think that if they call the priest all hope will be gone. But that is the exact opposite of what the anointing means.

Of course it's understandable if relatives don't want to frighten someone who is gravely ill, thinking he will lose all will to live. But that can only happen if the person has already a false idea of what the anointing of the sick means. The best thing is for the sick person to remove all anxiety from his relatives and friends by asking for the anointing himself. That should be the normal thing — not the anointing at the last minute. It is usually combined with confession and communion, and it is essential that the person should be conscious.

It is best not to leave a sick person alone during the anointing but to pray with him and accept his witness of faith. Then the common hope of all Christians in resurrection with Jesus will be apparent.

If a Christian should die in special circumstances without having received the anointing, there is no need to worry. What is important is his faith in resurrection with Jesus Christ.

16

Do we still need priests?

Once upon a time the priesthood was a vocation for intelligent believing Christians who wanted to help their fellow Christians. They had a lot of work but they could get through it. Churches were full. Their words and their advice were listened to. They received a lot of love and certainly much respect. Their greatest joy was baptizing children and then seeing them grow in faith helped by their words and assistance in faith; seeing them receiving the other sacraments, growing up, marrying and themselves bringing their children to baptism. Priests were the pillars of their parishes, and the parishes were their priests' support.

Priests today

Today things are different. Churches aren't full. The priests' words and advice are as valid as the degree of conviction their reasoning seems to carry. Instead of love and respect they are often greeted with amusement and contempt. They seldom watch a person growing up in faith; on the contrary they watch people escaping priestly influence. Since parishes have changed into more complex things because of the widespread changes in society, priests have much more to do and find it less possible to get through all their tasks. They can't be jacks of all trades. The priesthood is no longer something to dream about. Others often satisfy men's needs more effectively.

Many priests nowadays are uncertain. They often say so and try to make changes that answer the demands made on the Church today. In the meantime the number of priests gets smaller and smaller. To understand their worries we must understand why we need them.

Preaching the good news

A priest isn't a higher-ranking Christian. He has to believe, hope and love like all other Christians. He falls into sin in the same way and has to ask for forgiveness like all other Christians. The sacraments he administers are things he is just as much in need of as the others. The word of God he preaches and explains is something he has to listen to most attentively and take to heart. His ordination doesn't give him a privileged position at the Last Judgment. We mustn't put him on an altar. The only thing that makes a priest different from all the rest of us is his special task.

The second Vatican Council described his task when it said that the people of God were united primarily by the word of the living God which is sought from the priest. Since no one can be saved without faith it is the first task of priests, as assistants of the bishops, to announce the good news to all men. The Council insists that the administration of the sacraments is included in the preaching of the word, because the sacraments visibly embody the word of God and are always bound up with the pronouncement of that word. Therefore it is the task of a priest to unite the community by preaching the gospel and administering the sacraments. Priests do that as the bishops' assistants, which means that the president of the parish or community is properly a bishop. Since bishops can't be everywhere at once, priests work on the spot.

Changes in the ministry

We need priests like that. Christian belief and community of faith in the Church are impossible if no one tells us about God, about Jesus and about our salvation, and if no one sees that divine service is held. That cannot be left to chance. Therefore certain Christians are priests not by individual right, but are commissioned, named and sent. That was the case in the New Testament. If we read the letters of Paul we see how the apostle commissioned his fellow workers and sent them into the communities. Even though the individual ministries have changed in the Church they arose from that basic form we find in the New Testament: the first bearers of Christ's commission in the Church — the twelve disciples of Jesus, the witnesses of the resurrection, called others to work with them, and sent them out; and they did the same, and so on right up to the present day.

Why then is there a crisis of the priesthood? In the triangle of tasks performed by the priest, in leading the parish or another community, preaching and administering the sacraments, two areas have changed. The parishes are different today, members of the community live differently, and therefore the way in which the word is to be preached to them has to be different too.

Even catechists and social workers, parish councils and many parishioners have taken over tasks which a priest had to do himself, in earlier times. The process will continue. The Church has to take care that the good news is brought to all Christians as *they* need it. Perhaps those parishioners who do secondary jobs which were formerly a priest's duty will be ordained to the priesthood so that they can also assist the leader of the parish in their particular area by administering the sacraments. We should welcome such a development. The Church needs as many priests as are necessary to bring the word and the sacraments to men and women.

Ordination

Ordination is a celebration and service in which the bishop lays his hands on a Christian and thereby publicly entrusts him with the tasks of a priest. The laying on of hands occurs in the New Testament (Acts 13. 3; I Timothy 4. 14; 2 Timothy 1. 6). In its own way – in regard to service in the parish or other community – ordination has all the marks of a sacrament, and therefore the Catholic Church counts it as one of its seven sacraments.

The Church insists that there is only *one* leader and "bishop" in the Church: Jesus Christ himself. Therefore he is known too as the "Head" of the Church (see Ephesians 1. 22; 5. 23; Colossians 1. 18). If the earthly bishop commissions and ordains a parish leader, a priest, he does so because he is convinced that Jesus himself has called this Christian to that office. Therefore the Church cannot undertake to release from his office a Christian whom Jesus himself has chosen. Anyone who is ordained a priest remains a priest for the rest of his life, even if he is released from his duties in a particular parish, or "laicized", or dismissed.

As with other sacraments, Protestant Churches also recognize ordination, though not always as a "sacrament" proper. And the Churches of the Reformation usually ordain a man for his whole life too.

Priest and parish

If a priest is "only" commissioned and sent and isn't a higher-level sort of Christian, is there any reason to respect the priest as people used to? Yes, but the deep respect should be for the office. And respect should also be paid to the courage of a man who undertakes such a task. If an ordinary Christian without any office in the Church has difficulties in his faith, that doesn't really affect anyone beyond those very close to him. He can in a sense wait patiently while he works things through. But things are different for a priest. What is to be done if he has to preach and live the faith and yet sees more shadows of doubt than light? And can any priest be certain when he's ordained that that won't happen to him?

A priest risks a lot of testing situations in his lifetime. Today especially he is subject to a number of crises. But no trial or crisis, not even the trial of celibacy (which in the Roman Catholic Church is still a condition of the exercise of the priesthood), is as bad as the rift between the duty of preaching the gospel and the experience of a personal crisis of faith. Men who take the risk of that kind of trial – for our sake – deserve respect.

No Old Testament prophet suffered as much from the burden of his divine duty as Jeremiah. But on one occasion he accused God: "O Lord, thou hast deceived me, and I was deceived; thou art stronger than I, and thou has prevailed. I have become a laughingstock all the day; everyone mocks me. For whenever I speak, I cry out, I shout: 'Violence and destruction!' . . . If I say: 'I will not mention him, or speak any more in his name,' there is in my heart as it were a burning fire shut up in my bones, and I am weary with holding it in, and I cannot" (Jeremiah 20. 7-9). Something of this is experienced nowadays by every priest, every bishop, every deacon, and everyone who has an office in the Church — if he takes his duty seriously.

17

Should the Church proclaim dogmas?

One of the main differences between the Catholic and Protestant Churches seems to be that the Catholic Church "issues" dogmas or things to be believed, and that Catholics think that such dogmas are issued by the "magisterium" or teaching authority of the Church under the guidance of the Holy Spirit without error; whereas Protestants on the whole reject the magisterium and dogmas. Outwardly that seems to be the case, but the difference is often misinterpreted, for instance when people think that Catholics automatically believe, at Rome's command, whereas Protestants can believe as they think right. It isn't so simple.

Dogmas can be necessary
A dogma is a prouncement of faith that the Church holds to be essential, so that you can't be a Christian if you deny it. Therefore the Church proclaims it solemnly. For a long time now that has been done by ecumenical Councils: that is, through the assembly of all Catholic bishops of the world (who have asked advice from theologians and members of their dioceses beforehand), or in exceptional cases by the Pope alone as successor of the Apostle Peter and chief bishop of the whole Church and President of a Council. But the first forms of a dogma (" dogma" is a Greek word and means "teaching" or "doctrine") are to be found in the New Testament. Paul writes to the Romans: "If you confess with your lips that Jesus is Lord and believe in your heart that God raised him from the dead, you will be saved" (Rom. 10. 9). And in the first epistle of John we read: "By this you know the Spirit of God: every spirit which confesses that Jesus Christ has come in the flesh is of God, and every spirit which does not confess Jesus is not of God" (1 John 4. 2-3). Both therefore hold that certain beliefs or propositions are essential if one is to be "saved", to be "of God", to be a Christian: "Jesus is Lord", "God raised him from the

dead", "Jesus Christ has come in the flesh" – these are dogmas from the New Testament.

At times they are necessary. When men accept faith, they also begin to think about the gospel message, some more than others, according to ability. That is understandable. But no one can stop some things coming out of this process of reflection which encourage confusion or error. Above all when people try to adjust the gospel of faith to the spirit of the times. Things often readjust themselves. For example, when a theologian "goes too far", there is sure to be another who offers good reasons for rejecting the error he has detected. Usually every theologian takes great care to search out good reasons for his propositions and does not light-heartedly emit new teachings all the time. In fact it is difficult to exceed the boundaries of Christian faith. Even when we see, read or listen to theologians in apparently fierce and contradictory argument about questions of faith, they have to go a very long way before either of the parties to the debate has left the safe ground of faith.

Dogmas have limits

But the limits can be exceeded. The confusion can be so great that the leaders of the Church, the Pope and bishops, have to do something to ensure that the faithful are not weakened in their faith. That is how the dogmas of the New Testament were formulated. The apostles as it were said to their faithful: If anyone says that thing, he isn't preaching the Christian faith with you have learned. Faith says the following . . .

1. A dogma is a marking out of boundaries. It says: Go this far and no further, if you want to be a Christian, for no one can force you to believe. No dogma replaces further thought or forbids it. A Christian not only has to state what isn't his faith, but above all what his faith *is* and means for mankind.

2. In its language a dogma is always bound to a particular time. The debate and definition can be completely incomprehensible at a later date. When for example the Council of Chalcedon – a town in present-day Turkey – proclaimed in 451 the dogma that there were two natures in Jesus – the divine and the human – everyone know what was meant. We hardly understand it today. At least we would put it quite differently. But what the dogma *means*, that is something that we understand very well.

3. No dogma can express all the truth of faith with all its riches. Dogmas too are like windows which all look into a beautiful tree in a big court-yard. The same tree is seen through every window, and yet everyone sees something different from each window, because one sees an aspect of the tree that can't be seen from the other windows.

Dogmas occur less often than we think

Due proclamation of a dogma is a very difficult thing and due holding of past dogmas isn't easy. Some people always want them to be kept word for word (such people are often called "conservatives") and others want something more advanced, something new, to be said (they are often called progressive). Admittedly a number of mistakes were made in the past in proclaiming dogmas. Decisions were made too quickly, not enough thought went into judgments. Sometimes power interests and pride crept into the proclamation of a dogma. But the profit that dogmas have brought to the Church is greater. By means of clear teaching decisions binding on the whole Church and difficult crises have been overcome and millions of Christians have been confirmed in their faith. Sometimes Protestant Christians envy Catholics their degree of certitude.

On the other hand, the absence of a Protestant Pope doesn't mean that there is no teaching authority in the Protestant Churches. Protestants usually believe that in the course of time, by discussion and debate, the Holy Spirit will bring the truth to light. The Catholic Church believes that in certain cases of necessity a decision made by those who carry responsibility in the Church on Jesus's behalf can make the truth certain for the faithful, because the guidance of the Holy Spirit is behind all such ventures.

Apart from such special cases, the ways in which the truth of faith is kept and remains in force in the different Churches, are not so dissimilar as it at first seems. Dogmas aren't announced every day in the Catholic Church. A proper understanding of faith is largely arrived at by fair debate among theologians, careful guidance by bishops and other leaders, and above all by the living practice of faith by every Christian. Nothing could be less exact than the claim that a dogma is an order from the church bosses which the faithful have to follow blindly. The dogma expresses what the faith of the Church is – what *our* faith is. No Pope can proclaim a dogma which he knows beforehand is not accepted by the majority of Catholic Christians.

How many dogmas are there?

It is very doubtful that the Church would use dogmas as much as in the past, in order to settle disputes. The second Vatican Council issued a number of decrees but never proclaimed a single dogma. The world and human questions have now become so complex that no church leader can assume that everything important has already been thought of, considered, and pronounced upon.

Sometimes people ask: How many dogmas are there? That is hard to say, for many have been announced with different words. A rule of thumb is possible: Dogma in the Catholic Church is found in the Nicene creed, for it joins the apostolic confession of faith to the decisions of the first general councils. There are seven sacraments through which God strengthens our faith and sends us his grace. Among the seven sacraments, the Eucharist is most prominent, because Christ himself is present under the forms of bread and wine. The Church, and its offices and the capacities of its office-holders, are no human arrangement, but willed by Jesus and established by divine proxy.

18

Can the Churches unite?

If the major divisions of the western Christian Church remain exactly as they are today, thinking of themselves and one another exactly as they do, they can't unite in *one* Church yet. If they tried to do so the result would be inauthentic. The Churches are united enough in their belief.

Dialogue between the Churches
But the fact that the Churches can't unite as yet doesn't mean that the separation is the same as it was for centuries. The times are long past when nothing but suspicion, rejection, criticism, contempt and even hatred stood between the Churches, and when they didn't even talk to one another. In this century, and mainly after the second World War, dialogue or talk between the Churches has made incredible progress. Catholic and Protestant theologians have looked carefully into the old disputes and have discovered that in many cases the Churches merely misunderstood one another and even exaggerated things in some cases so as to continue the alienation between the denominations.

At the second Vatican Council and at several important assemblies of the Protestant Churches or Churches of the Reformation, this common work has been recognized in a way that would have seemed inconceivable fifty years ago. When Catholic and Protestant theologians discuss important questions of faith nowadays, it is often impossible to tell which are Catholics and which Protestants. The second Vatican Council called the Protestants or Reformed Christians, Anglicans, Episcopalians and so on, "Churches" whereas in the past the word "Church" would have been avoided in this regard. Broad agreement has been reached (for instance between Catholics and Anglicans and Catholics and Methodists) about the nature of the Eucharist or Holy Orders, and open discussions are held about reciprocal recognition of Orders and general admission to communion at the Eucharist, the Mass, or the Lord's Supper of different Churches.

This progress has been possible even though theologians and other members of the Churches are warned against too great haste in jumping the hurdle of continuing differences in belief. One particularly difficult problem now seems almost to have been solved. Anyway people don't get hot under the collar about it as they did in the past: and that is the question of "mixed" or inter-church marriages. The personal decision in full conscience of the people who are getting married is now widely respected, and the grim warnings and threats of the past have now vanished for the most part.

Unresolved questions

In spite of all this progress some questions are unresolved. At present it does not seem that the Protestant Churches will ever recognize the Papacy as the Catholic Church understands it — however "humanely" and sympathetically the Pope may exercise his office. Some of them will not adopt and acknowledge the sacraments as they are recognized by Catholics apart from baptism and the Eucharist, and not all are ready to understand the Eucharist in anything like the Catholic sense of the representation of Christ's sacrifice. Protestants are generally reluctant to pray to Mary and the saints, however much the Catholic Church distances itself from past excesses in this direction. They also seem unprepared to take the same interest in the nature of marriage and responsibility for it that is common in the Catholic Church. And of course most Catholics will not accept Protestant ideas on these subjects and a few others.

Mutual enrichment

Therefore it seems only truthful for the Churches not to unite at the moment. There are not just questions of dispute between them but differences in devotional practice and church life. Of course differences were and are not in themselves reasons for continuing the division between the Churches, but they are historical facts. These different forms of practice are wholly Christian, and of great value to Christian faith, yet history has decreed their location in one or the other Church.

For instance, there is the typically evangelical Protestant joy in the Bible; in praying the psalms, and the many wonderful hymns which Catholics are only now beginning to learn; the profound conviction that we are sinners, that we have to hope in God's mercy and should not trust in ourselves to too great an extent; and there is a great inner sense of freedom to tackle the problems of this world often more courageously than Catholics do. On the Catholic side there is a greater degree of joy in parish services, in the liturgy, the sacraments, the many traditional forms of prayer which are still alive among Catholics and from which each can choose a method of devotion that suits him; and there is the profound joy which does not reject all that is beautiful in the world but adopts it for divine service, even when it is not a Christian "discovery": candles, colours, images, perfume (incense), water; and or course a readiness to place under God's blessing everything of importance in man's life, from the harvest field to the motor car. In addition belief in each Church has something like its own "style" or atmosphere which is difficult to describe but immediately perceptible in radio sermons and so on.

A lot of the things I've just mentioned have already been adopted reciprocally by various Churches or parts of them. But much that is of value is still restricted to one or the other Church. Who will guarantee that in the eventuality of union or reunion some of those unique ideas and practices won't be abandoned for ever just in order to hasten the process. So long as we can't be sure that the richness and variety of Christian life preserved in all the Churches will be taken over into a united Church without any loss, then — quite apart from major questions of faith — it is better for the Churches to preserve and deepen their own living inheritance.

Working together

It is very important that Catholic, Protestant and Orthodox Christians should work together in their neighbourhoods. It is very important for them to get to know one another. They should discuss faith and differences of faith together, but more often how to live a life of faith, how to pray and how to give children a religious education. If you're a Catholic, go to a Protestant service and compare it with your own. What is different? What is better or worse? Ask the priests and ministers to arrange common services and meetings whenever possible. Everything that can be done in common should be done: marriage counselling, educational guidance, social welfare, immigrant English and literacy courses, aid for down-and-outs, and so on, exchange of religious education teachers, and well-prepared and interesting services. And of course every possible common effort should be made to stamp out sectarian preferences at work and to remove all possible causes of inter-denominational dissension.

19

Do we have to pray every day?

We have said "daily prayers" since we were little. When we confess our sins, the list of faults and omissions in our prayer-book or in our mind asks us if we have neglected our daily prayers or said them unthinkingly. Yet we tend to find these prayers rather a burden. Do we really have to pray every day?

Everyday prayers
By everyday prayers I mean morning and evening prayers and prayers at meals. They are a good custom and they shouldn't be given up without a good reason. But it is not a commandment of God that we should say morning, night and midday prayers. So it's no sin not to be able to say them or just not to say them. Instead we should ask why they can seem such a nuisance nowadays.

For a long time morning and night prayers were obvious practices for a Christian so long as work was arranged according to a simple day-and-night rhythm. People got up together and began the day with a prayer. They closed with a prayer before going to bed at the same time. And they prayed when they ate together. This custom also depended to some extent on the pattern of monastic life.

That simple rhythm has largely disappeared today. How can we say morning prayers properly when a modern household is like a beehive and everyone goes off to work one after the other? How can grace before and after meals be said when people seldom eat together? How is successful evening prayer possible when people quite justifiably want some leisure in the evening after work, if they go to the cinema or meet some friends for a night out.

Faith and prayer
Of course a Christian prays. Because he believes. For belief is the communion of man with God. If a man tries to express that faith he has

to say "you" and "I" and "we". So we call speaking *with* (not about) God prayer. The simplest and at the same time most important prayer, which sums up all other prayers, is "I believe in you". Belief itself is prayer, as soon as it is expressed in words.

Do we have to pray every day? That brings us to another question: Is it a good idea to express our faith in words every day, at least in a quite simple form? Yes, of course it is, even if we don't want to lay down any hard-and-fast rules. Anyone who works not only needs a free day some time in the week; he needs free time every day. Faith needs not only a major rest on Sunday, but a short time every day in order to be with God.

You can always make a sign of the cross, or say a "Glory be to the Father" or some other short prayer only a sentence long. Remember that no part of a man's life is as significant as that between sleeping and waking. You can say short prayers during the day too. They don't require much concentration and don't interrupt work. They can give a sense of union with God right in the middle of work. Formulas for the purpose can be taken from the liturgy: "Lord, have mercy"; "Your will be done"; "Give us peace"; "Hallowed be thy name"; "Give us our daily bread"; and so on.

You can also say in your own words whatever you want to tell God out of joy, thankfulness, care, awareness of guilt, and so on: "Lord, help me"; "Lord please help this man"; "Lord, I believe, save thou mine unbelief"; "Lord help me to bear this "; and above all: "Lord I believe in you".

If you pray like that you needn't worry about saying morning and evening prayers every day. On the other hand there are times every day when you can "switch off". Use them to say an Our Father, or a creed, or a psalm, or some other prayer.

Whenever you pray, if at all possible, read something from the Bible or a religious book that helps you with questions of faith.

20

What happens after death?

We ask for prospectuses and brochures to plan a holiday. They show what we are to expect in the best possible light. A marvellous hotel, terraces and patios and beaches where we can relax. Glittering tables in the dining room, the gorgeous sun . . . Just imagine if some quaint travel agent decided to put on the front of one of these leaflets a picture of a tumble-down hut in the middle of a swamp without any motor road, surrounded by jungle and lianas, with the question underneath this unappealing prospect: "Do you want to spend your holiday here. If not, then come to us!" What would that tell us about our holiday spot? No details — only that it's the opposite of what we see in the picture.

The situation is just as vague when as Christians we try to get a "prospect" of what awaits us after death. Paul writes: "The Lord Jesus Christ . . . will change our lowly body to be like his glorious body, by the power which enables him even to subject all things to himself" (Philippians 3. 21). We do not know what a glorified body is. But we do know what our lowly body is like. Very well. And that will be done with after death.

Eternal life
Faith tells us quite unambiguously what comes after death. All we need to do is to draw conclusions from what we already know.

We shall receive "eternal life": that means not only a life which never ceases, but a full life that is only life and no longer includes any trace of aging or the shadow of death. In short: a life like the life of God — as far as a creature can share in that.

We shall lead this life as *men*, not as pure spirits, but as beings of flesh and blood in whom everything spiritual is expressed in bodily terms and everything bodily is ruled by spirit and endowed with soul.

We shall not live each of us for ourselves but in communion with other men, especially with all those whom we have loved in this life.

Since we shall have died as human beings, eternal life will be granted to us only by God raising us up through his almighty creative power, as he raised Jesus from the dead.

Eternal life will be unending joy for us. And the external world will be so shaped that it too will be the basis and object of that joy. A sound and saved world, as God intended it for human beings; a world that men through sin put wrong and destroyed.

Unending joy will be possible because men will exist henceforth without any trace of self-glorification in communion with God. Whoever is right with God experiences the world quite differently. No longer as an inimical world, no longer as an invitation to self-glorification and domination, which then shatters into nothing, but as God's world entrusted to men to use and enjoy.

The judgment
The eternal life of mankind is the final victory of God's mercy over sin. Naturally that doesn't happen without man finally seeing the nature of his sin and renouncing it.

But after death nothing can spoil this vision of sin; nothing can any longer tempt a man to turn against God. In the sight of God man sees painfully his resistance to God as complete idiocy. This painful insight which makes men fit for a full life in the community of God is called, according to Scripture, the "judgement".

For Jesus's sake, God's mercy will be victorious in this judgment — even when in this life a man has not wholly broken with sin. And no man in his hour of death has wholly broken with sin. The only prerequisite for the mercy of God is that we should have believed during this life, and that means: accepted God's mercy. Whoever really refused that, didn't want it, will experience eternal life as eternal separation from God, and therefore eternal joylessness, eternal loneliness, an eternal death without eternal oblivion — in short: "hell".

Only images
Of course you will have noticed that everything faith has to say about life after death seems rather general. What does all that mean: "Full life", "resurrection", "joy", "redeemed world", "communion with God"? And aren't we faced with insoluble questions when for example we want to know where all these millions upon hundreds of millions of resurrected men could find room to live in this world, how a body will look which can no longer die, or when we recall the question which Jesus once posed: Who will a man be married to in eternity who was married several times on earth? (Mark 12. 18-27).

We really can't as yet concieve of the life that's intended for us. We can do only two things in order to make belief in eternal life somewhat clearer: We can first of all express our hope in pictures or *images*. Then, like Scripture, we shall have recourse to the best we are given on this earth, and imagine it increased everlastingly. In that way it becomes a simile for the joy of eternal life. Scripture has described eternal life in the imagery of an inconceivably immense marriage feast. Or as a city with golden and jewelled gates, in which there is no night. Or as a fantastically festive service with magnificent music. Or as peace over all the earth, in which even the animals share.

There is only one difficulty with such images. They depend to some extent on what the people who use them already find especially valuable and experience thus. In that way even the images of the Bible can cease to move us. The sort of situation can arise which might be summed up as people despising Christians for picturing eternal joy as singing in angelic choirs on cloud tops. We must remember that pictures are just pictures, and can never give more than an approximate idea of a reality that we have not yet seen. For that very reason we should try to find individual images which have something to say *to us*. For instance, surely we have a profound image of eternal life if we say: Then all men will love one another as they should do. Or: Then at last we shall have an answer to all the puzzling questions we can't solve now. Or: Then at last there will be proper compensation for the fact that many people here on earth have suffered terribly despite their complete lack of guilt and injustice, whereas others have never known need, and care and suffering.

Former things have passed away
We can also try to imagine everything shocking and evil and painful in this life, and then think of the exact opposite. Then we shall know in what direction our hope for eternal life should point. Scripture does that too. Paul for instance in the first letter to the Corinthians says that our life is weak, perishable and dishonourable, whereas we are intended to have a life that is imperishable, strong and glorious. (1 Corinthians 15. 42-3). And in the Revelation of John the Divine we read: "He will wipe away every tear from their eyes, and death shall be no more, neither shall there be mourning nor crying or pain any more, for the former things have passed away" (Revelation 21. 4). Surely, despite the poetic imagery, that is all quite clear?

Even when we don't any longer respond to any picture or comparison, then we should remember two sentences from the Bible: "For now we see in a mirror dimly, but then face to face" (1 Corinthians 13. 12). And: We shall be "at home with the Lord" (2 Corinthians 5. 8). To know that is enough.

And that should be enough. For the only guarantee of our hope in eternal life is Jesus, whom God has raised from the dead: the first of the resurrected. Because the resurrected Jesus exists we can say: "Now if Christ is preached as raised from the dead, how can some of you say that there is no resurrection of the dead? But if there is no resurrection of the dead, then Christ has not been raised; if Christ has not been raised then our preaching is in vain and your faith is in vain. . . .If for this life only we have hoped in Christ, we are of all men most to be pitied" (1 Corinthians 15. 12-13. 19).

21

Are Christians really free?

To be free. To shape our lives in freedom. That is one of the greatest ideals of our time. Sometimes people say that Christians, and above all Catholics, can't really be free. They are bound to all sorts of things which restrict their freedom or even abolish it. To the Bible, to the teaching of the Church, to divine commandments, to commandments of the Church, to conventions of church life, even to certain political options. Christians aren't free to think and behave as they wish.

Made free by Christ
We read in Galatians: "For freedom Christ has set us free; stand fast therefore, and do not submit again to a yoke of slavery" (Galatians 5. 1). Freedom is the very nature of Christian belief. To live in freedom is the duty of every Christian.

There are only two possibilities. If it is true that Christians can't be free, either the Church has fallen away from these words, or the opinion that Christians are necessarily unfree is incorrect.

We have to admit that freedom hasn't always been a universal mark of the Church. Even today, in spite of favourable developments in the last few centuries, the Church hasn't succeeded in inviting men to share in the freedom of the children of God. But that is to some extent inevitable. The Church has to emphasize the commandments of God, and a little pressure can easily become compulsion, backed up with ecclesiastical penalties and even the threat of eternal damnation. The Church has to organize a living community – a parish life. And what were at first good rules for getting along together can become burdens which hinder rather than help true faith.

The Church has to protect its children from temptation and error but not from conflicting opinions. That concern can easily turn into the repression of free research and opinion. The means for concern or

repression are always present in the Church. On the other hand the good
changes of the last few decades show that the Church is trying to follow
the standard proclaimed by Paul in Galatians. We hope that the process
will be more thorough in future.

True and apparent freedom

We cannot say that the Church has "degenerated" from the standard of
Galatians. And we can say that the opinion that Christian belief necessarily makes one unfree is wholly false. Surely there is no need for me to
prove that at the end of this book. I only have to recall what I said in chapters 1 to 3 and 7 to 9. Is "freedom" licence — permission to do and allow
whatever I wish? Is unfreedom attachment to values and moral demands?
If it is so then we hardly need to refute it. Such "freedom" is only
slavery to the false god of oneself. And that false god keeps no promises.
He falls back into the very slavery from which he promised release.

No freedom is merely greater than the freedom of belief in God who
is the source of all freedom. He takes away our worry about the meaning
of our existence. We can let anything happen, for the man who knows
that he is held in the hollow of God's hand cannot lose his way.

God liberates us to love, through belief in his love, and through the
commandments which show us the way. Because we no longer have to
care for ourselves, we are set free from egotism and can turn with all
our strength towards the people whom we have to serve because we
want to serve them.

God has freed our reason so that we can live in the community without care for our personal advantage, and so that we can devise rules for
communal life in our society and in the Church — rules which create
the necessary balance to prevent anyone from exercising his freedom at
another's cost. God has also given us the freedom to oppose human laws
which contradict the law of God. A conscience enlightened by faith will
never confuse the mere laws of man with the laws of God, which alone
give life. Finally God has made us so free that we can even bear futility,
and eventually the ultimate futility, which is death. A Christian knows
through the cross and resurrection of Jesus that death is not the last
word. Therefore he has no fear of death.

The good news

Who is freer than a Christian? Everything which seems to restrict his
freedom is either the very basis of his freedom or connected with it (the
Bible, or doctrine); or it has to do with life in freedom (commandments,
or community rules). The real obstacles to his freedom are only forms
of disloyalty to the Christian message. That can happen, but it is no
argument against faith. Faith has to oppose such abuses for its own sake.

But freedom is a duty of faith. Paul is quite sure of that. If anyone feels unfree in his faith, something is very wrong: either with him, or with the way in which faith is presented — brought close — to him.

What Paul says is a summary of all faith and a standard for any Christian life and for the life of the Church: "For freedom Christ has set us free; stand fast therefore, and do not submit again to a yoke of slavery" (Galatians 5. 1). There is no reason to be ashamed of this good news in our modern world.